Your Seventh Sense

How To Think Like A Comedian

Your Seventh Sense

© 2006 by Karyn Ruth White and Jay Arthur
ISBN 1-884180-72-2
   978-1-884180-27-2

Published by LifeStar
2244 S. Olive St.
Denver, CO 80224-2518
(888) 468-1535 or (303) 757-2039 (orders only)
(888) 468-1537 or (303) 753-9355 (phone)
(888) 468-1536 or (303) 753-9675 (fax)

For program inquiries:

Keynote Programs:
Contact Karyn Ruth White at 1-877-KRWHITE or visit www.karynruthwhite.com

Training Programs:
Contact Jay Arthur at 1-888-468-1537 or www.qimacros.com

www.yourseventhsense.com

Your Seventh Sense
Contents

Life is a tragedy when seen in close-up, but it's a comedy in long-shot.

CHARLIE CHAPLIN

PREFACE

Humor is just another defense against the universe.
Mel Brooks

People come to us and say, "I know my life is off balance when I've lost my sense of humor." Your humor is a precious thing that needs to be nurtured, cared for, guarded and valued. So, first and foremost, know that your sense of humor is a priority. It needs to be fed and nurtured just like every other aspect of your health. This book was written to help you develop and expand your Seventh Sense – your sense of humor.

It seems to get more and more difficult to maintain your sense of humor in a world that takes itself WAY too seriously. The headlines and 24-hour news channels provide a constant barrage of messages of death and destruction. And just when you're feeling that there is nothing left to laugh about, an eighty-year-old woman in a gold polyester jumpsuit passes you in the grocery aisle and you lose it! This is the universe's way of telling you that tragedy and comedy live side by side.

People have trouble conceptualizing the idea that tragedy and comedy are inextricably bound together. We are brought up in an either/or society. We tend to be linear thinkers, but life isn't linear, it's circular and convoluted. Life refuses to be pigeonholed. Have you ever had a situation that was very serious and, in the middle of dealing with it, you found something hilarious to laugh about? It seems that those in professions with the highest stress levels (e.g., police, fire fighters, paramedics, health care professionals and even funeral directors) often have well-defined, playful, albeit sometimes morbid, senses of humor which help them cope with the tragedies they deal with every day. Laughing is one of the greatest human release valves for pent up stress, anxiety and fear.

Obviously not everything is fodder for funny, but a large slice of life can be viewed through a "funny lens" if we allow ourselves to go there.

Karyn Ruth's friend, Alison, was in her third year of battling breast cancer. She was sitting in her doctor's office waiting for yet another test result when the nurse approached her and said, "Dr. Barth will be right with you." Alison's husband, Marv (a man with a highly-honed Seventh Sense), said, "Dr. Who?" The nurse repeated, "Dr. Barth." Alison and Marv then proceeded to go into a sidesplitting routine about a dog with a lisp and they were "barthing" themselves silly when the doctor walked in. They were like two little kids rolling on the floor with laughter. This story reminds us that if we are willing to look, humor can be found in even the direst of circumstances.

Here's another great Marv and Alison story: Marv proposed to Alison over breakfast one morning. She said she couldn't possibly give him an answer that minute because she had a big real estate test that afternoon and she needed to concentrate. Only after she took her test did the realization hit her that Marv had actually proposed to her. She ran to the nearest pay phone, called him and yelled, "YES! YES! YES!" Marv, in an understated voice said, "Yes what?" She said, "Yes, I'll marry you!" Marv replied, "That's great ...who is this?"

Humor is a matter of perspective. It only took a few days after 9-11 for Leno's and Letterman's writers to start finding ways to poke fun at Osama Bin Laden. That's what comedians do; they find ways to turn tragedy into comedy. Tragedy is a hard pill to swallow, but humor helps coat the pill, making it easier to swallow. That's powerful.

The mission of this book is to make you laugh while teaching you about humor. We want you to finish this book with a better understanding and appreciation of *your* sense of humor – what it's all about and how you can use it effectively.

This book is unique in that it combines the science of Neuro-Linguistic Programming (NLP) along with the artistry of stand-up comedy to help the average person learn to attract and create humor. Jay Arthur has been studying comedians and humorists for over 10 years, and has concentrated on the science of humor. Karyn Ruth White has been writing and performing stand-up comedy for over 20 years and has honed the art of humor. Together we'll walk you step-by-step through the humor-making process.

We hope that the user-friendly principles we've provided throughout the book will inspire you to cherish, broaden and exercise your wonderful sense of humor. Heaven knows, the world needs all the humor it can get.

NLP AND YOUR SEVENTH SENSE

Neuro-Linguistic Programming (NLP) began its development in the early 1970s. At its core, NLP allows you to study experts or geniuses "doing their thing" in their natural habitats, and helps you figure out how they run their minds in order to create results and achieve success.

In the early days, this technique allowed Richard Bandler, John Grinder, and Robert Dilts to decode the skills of the extremely successful psychotherapists Milton Erickson, Virginia Satir, and Fritz Perls. Most of what passes for NLP today is training on these therapeutic techniques. But the heart of NLP is much more than that.

Once you understand how an expert or a genius thinks, you can decode their mental software and install it in your own head to get similar results. Then you can design training to install the expert/genius-level software in the minds of others. This is the power of NLP. The process of observing, analyzing, distilling, decoding, and installing the best mental software is called *modeling*.

In the past, modeling has been used for everything from learning spelling strategies (i.e., see the word in your mind's eye) to winning at poker, to trading commodities. When Jay began to study comedians, it became clear to him that comedians think differently than most people. So in this book, we want to model how comedians and humorists think, because laughter is a vital key to reducing stress, increasing health, being more creative, and living a better life.

The first step in modeling is simply to observe experts doing or talking about their specialty. This involves more than just listening to their words. As we all know, people rarely speak without using gestures or physical movements. A posture or tilt of the head can be more important than the words someone says. Similarly, the eyes may be windows into the soul, but they are also windows into a person's mental programming. When people look up, they are usually remembering or creating visual pictures in their minds. When they look down and to their right, they are often accessing their feelings. NLP offers, a highly refined set of filters for observing a genius at work and for capturing the nuances of their mental software.

All mental software is made up of pictures, sounds, feelings, smells, and tastes. While we normally think of the five senses as external experiences, the mind can remember or construct them without any "real" external stimulation at all. If you don't believe it, think of a lemon. Do you see a color and a shape? Can you feel its texture? Can you smell it? Can you taste it?

Unlike computer software which is totally on/off and yes/no in its construction, the five senses are more flexible. Pictures can get closer or farther away, bigger and brighter or smaller and dimmer. They can be in color or in black-and-white, sharp or fuzzy, and so on. The same flexibility is true for sounds, feelings, smells and tastes.

The modeler's job is to decode all of these internal and external representations offered by the expert and sift through them for the key pieces of mind-code that can deliver the results. While you and I may never fully understand all of the nuances of an expert's craft, we can easily grasp the essence or the core of his or her craft. The core of genius is always simple and elegant; it's never complex. There is always a logic or sequence used to achieve a certain goal or accomplish a certain task. There are beliefs and values that support ability. If we break the overall ability down into smaller chunks that can be taught in a logical sequence, then anyone can learn to do anything – maybe not at the expert level initially, but certainly well beyond a beginner level.

This is exactly how Jay began to study comedians. He watched comedians talking about their craft on The Comedy Channel; he took a five-week comedy class from Karyn Ruth; he studied other humorists he knew in the

National Speakers Association. As he watched all of these comedians doing their thing, a pattern emerged. He noticed a certain sequence they all followed to find the humor in any given situation. He "tried it on" until he got the basic working parts installed in his mental tool kit. He then approached Karyn Ruth and proposed teaching some comedy classes together to try to transfer these abilities to other people, tuning up the training model as they went along. The result is this book and the Seventh Sense Workshops.

Installing mental software can be easy and fun. Normally, we call this "learning." Unfortunately, many of us have learned to associate "learning" with sitting at uncomfortable desks and listening to boring presentations. But learning doesn't have to be painful. It would be great if we all had CD-ROM drives in our foreheads so we could simply install mental software directly, but we don't (yet). And sometimes you have to uninstall your current mental software (the buggy software) before you can effectively install and run the expert software. This is another core capability that NLP modeled early on: how to create experiential exercises that simplify and streamline the transfer and installation of genius level mental software.

It doesn't matter what field of endeavor you choose, modeling with NLP can explore and decode the essence of any human skill or ability. Humor is one of those abilities.

It takes time to build your humor muscle. Neurologists have found that the brain will rewire itself if you practice something often enough. They call this process *neuroplasticity*. Your brain may already seem hard-wired, but it can rewire itself with your help. That's why changing a habit takes 21 days. After 21 days of doing it differently, your brain begins to rewire itself. A bad habit is just neuroplasticity gone bad. So why not start building some good habits?

If you would like to know more about NLP, go to the Resources section at the end of this book for suggested reading.

When I die
I want to go like my
Grandfather did;
peacefully in his
sleep, not screaming
like the other
passengers in his car.

UNKNOWN

CHAPTER ONE
CAN ANYONE BE FUNNY?

A person without a sense of humor is like a wagon without springs, jolted by every pebble in the road.

Henry Ward Beecher

"Can you learn to be funny or is it something you're born with?" We believe the answer is, yes and yes!

James Lipton, host of The Actors Studio, asked Robin Williams that question. Williams said, "It's about 50/50." Half innate talent and half learned skill. So, if you want to be a stand-up comedian, it helps to have an innate sense of what's funny, a natural flair for seeing the humor in everyday life, and funny parents. But if you just want to add a little more fun and laughter to your daily life, there is a science to humor, as well as an art.

There is a structure, sequence and logic to this art form, and anyone can learn it and apply it. First, let's take a look at some of the old programming that may be blocking your Seventh Sense.

UNLEARNING OLD PROGRAMMING

The average preschool child laughs over 400 times a day, while the average adult laughs 15 times. We seem to lose our ability to laugh as the years advance.

My father always yelled when he was getting ready for work. "Where the hell is my shirt? Why can't I ever find my damn shoes? Why don't I have any friggin' clean socks?" I finally asked, "Mom, why does Dad always have to yell in the morning?" She said, "Oh Honey, he can't help it. Your father's always been a cross dresser."

KARYN RUTH WHITE

Do you remember laughing as a kid and getting in trouble for it? Do you remember your parents saying, "Finish your homework/chores/spinach and *then* you can go out to play," when you were growing up? Parents systematically taught us that work and play are two separate things, and that play can not occur until the work is done. As a result, we grow into adults who compartmentalize the concepts of work and play. As an adult, the work is *never* done, so when is it time for play? If you watch a child, you soon notice that work and play are inseparable. There is no separation of the two concepts in a child's mind.

Throughout our childhoods, someone is always telling us, "Get serious! Stop being silly! Wipe that smile right off your face!" We constantly receive messages that humor and laughter are not okay or that they are inappropriate. We are made to believe that we are somehow being disrespectful to the world at large by daring to express our humor. It gets to the point that we start to believe this nonsense on some very deep level. With this type of unchallenged programming, is it any wonder we have lost touch with our Seventh Sense? So how do you start the process of getting back in touch? How do you start to reprogram your mind to embrace humor rather than censor it?

First, realize that you were programmed to think about humor in a certain way. You were either rewarded for it or punished for it. Just as every classroom had a class clown who was rewarded by his peers for making people laugh, those classrooms also had a quiet or even sullen child whose humor had been repressed. Which one best describes you?

To reprogram yourself to find the funny in everyday life, work and relationships, you will need to understand

Don't you love getting older? Remember when you thought "incontinent" was a geographical term?

KARYN RUTH WHITE

how you think about humor and why it's important to you. And in order to do that, you need to get in touch with your inner thoughts about humor. This process is about helping *you* get in touch with *your* unique sense of humor.

HOW DO YOU DEFINE HUMOR?

First, let's define what humor means to you. For stand-up comedians, humor is a highly refined art form. They can tell you instantly if something is funny or not. For the rest of us, it may just be a newspaper headline or a cartoon that strikes us as funny.

Exercise: Start your own Seventh Sense Journal and list and answer the following questions:

- How do I define humor or comedy?
- Where, when and with whom do I believe it is appropriate and useful?
- Where is it inappropriate?
- Where could I use more humor in my life?
- Where and when do I lose my sense of humor?

(Note: Continue to use your Seventh Sense Journal as an aid for completing the exercises throughout this book, or use the Notes pages in the back of the book.)

Humor can be used in almost any situation to lessen the stress and increase our ability to deal with life's many challenges. If you study comedians, you'll find that most came from difficult neighborhoods and families. David Brenner said he was a gang leader and that he used humor to defuse confrontations with other gangs. Humor is an essential tool for coping with tragedy, stupidity, frustration, disappointment or whatever else life throws at you.

"Spell Check"
is like a man.
Don't be afraid
to use it,
but never count on it
entirely.

KARYN RUTH WHITE

WHY IS HUMOR IMPORTANT TO YOU?

Getting clear on why humor is important to you will help you to anchor it as a core value in your life. You wouldn't take the time and effort attracting and creating more humor in your life if you didn't genuinely value it. Right? Sometimes a great way to reaffirm this value is to ask yourself, "Why is humor important to me?"

Here are some of the answers our Seventh Sense Workshop students came up with when asked:

WHY IS HUMOR IMPORTANT TO YOU?

- Humor actually makes my life better.
- My job is very stressful. When I remember to use humor on the job it makes my job easier and I get along better with my coworkers.
- I'd rather laugh with my spouse than fight.
- My kids are at an age where they take everything so seriously. I want to help them lighten up.
- It's magnetic. I've noticed that a good sense of humor really draws people to you. I use it whenever I am in new social situations.
- I can't really explain it, but humor just seems to make my life flow better.
- My sales go better. I seem to close a lot of sales deals when I interject humor.

Exercise: In your Seventh Sense Journal, make a list of reasons why humor is important to you. Keep this list handy so you can look at it as a reminder when life tries to zap you of your humor. Keeping a close connection to your Seventh Sense takes a conscious effort because life will challenge it almost every day.

I recently broke up
with a man I was
dating.
He wasn't able to give
me the one thing I
needed in a
relationship...
eye contact.

KARYN RUTH WHITE

WHAT DID YOU LEARN ABOUT HUMOR?

We can't reprogram new thoughts until we know our existing thoughts. Once you've had the opportunity to get in touch with your innermost beliefs about humor, ask yourself whether or not these beliefs are truly yours or whether you have accepted them unquestioned from the other sources in your life. This is where the process gets exciting. You now have an opportunity to challenge these long-held beliefs and in doing so, make room for some new ones.

Think about how humor was used in your house growing up. Was there a lot of humor or none? Were you encouraged to use humor or were you punished for it? Close your eyes and remember the family sitting around the dinner table. Was humor allowed or did you sit in silence? How did your parents use and value humor?

Exercise: In your Seventh Sense Journal, write about what you remember learning about humor. What messages did you internalize from your family and teachers? Sometimes getting your thoughts down on paper helps to give you a new perspective on your thinking and your beliefs. This new perspective can then pave the way for some new thinking and behavior.

HOW WE DEFINE HUMOR

POSITIVE VERSUS NEGATIVE HUMOR

There is a lot of confusion about exactly what humor is and is not. Humor can be used positively, or it can be used as a sword. We live in a world in which many comedians use humor as a sword rather than as an olive branch. We

Absolutely no credit! You should have known yesterday that you'd be hungry today.

SIGN IN COUNTRY DINER

are subjected to a lot of vulgar humor in Western society. A lot of anger is masked as humor. Anger and hostility masked as humor are a coward's way of dealing with life. After all, rudeness is just a weak person's attempt at strength.

COMEDY IS WAR

Consider the terminology used in the comedy world: I slayed. I killed. I destroyed. And if you don't do well, "I died or I bombed." This is the language of war. Comedy is war, and war is hell. So comedy must be hell, right? It doesn't have to be.

Granted, comedy is an aggressive sport, but in everyday usage you can get your point across without belittling or alienating anyone. People are much more apt to accept what you have to tell them if it's not delivered in an intimidating, degrading, authoritative, or patronizing way. Effective humor is not about one-upping another person, nor is it about becoming the victim. It's about healing the situation and connecting with the other person. If you can use humor in a good-hearted way, people are more likely to accept what you have to say. They can hear your message without feeling like they've lost a part of themselves in the process. That is hugely powerful.

Humor, in its highest form, should always be a point of connection between people. Humor should be a path to healing. In our book, humor is always defined as a good-hearted and loving (sometimes mischievous) attempt to connect people through common experience and humanity.

HUMOR IN THE FRIENDLY SKIES

Jay was on a business flight and the flight attendant started doing the requisite safety announcement. She got

When I was a kid I wet my bed. It was embarrassing. Late one night I asked, "Mom, is there something wrong with me because I wet my bed every night?" She said, "No Honey, that's why they call them the wee wee hours of the morning."

KARYN RUTH WHITE

on the intercom and said, "Please pretend to pay attention to the Flight Attendant as she demonstrates the safety features of this airplane. In the event of an emergency, an oxygen mask will drop from the overhead compartment. When you stop screaming, place the mask over your nose and mouth and begin to breathe freely. Then put it over any children or people behaving like children sitting next to you."

Jay remembers thinking, *I never thought that you could make the safety instructions funny, but there it was and it was brilliant!*

"The whole plane just kind of lightened up. They were getting tense because we were late and the plane was hot. The flight attendant started doing this comedy bit and little chuckles started to ripple through the entire plane and pretty soon the anxiety was gone."

Humor is truly a magical thing. Humor really does get people's attention. People basically want to be entertained. Whether it's a student, an airline passenger, a businessperson, or an audience, they want to be entertained. It doesn't have to be knee-slapping hilarious, but if you can give someone something that is just a little off center, they may sit up a little straighter and pay attention. As Mary Poppins says, "Just a spoonful of sugar helps the medicine go down."

Humor is the sugar. It's just that little sugar coating that helps people to listen. Comedy plays a great role in transferring information from one mind to another.

Now that you know a little bit more about what you think about humor, let's explore what the professionals think. How do they orchestrate their thoughts to get laughs and find the funny in seemingly desolate territory?

You can turn painful situations around through laughter. If you can find humor in anything – even poverty – you can survive it.

BILL COSBY

CHAPTER TWO
HOW THE PROS THINK

Some I Just Do For Me

The world needs comedians. Comedians are the people who say what the rest of us are thinking. They take the unmentionable and mention it in an entertaining, thought-provoking, laugh-inducing way. They push the envelope and show us ourselves. They help keep us honest.

Comedians have the ability to step out of everyday life and observe it from an objective perspective. Then they blend their personal points of view with what they see. They then present their findings to the rest of us with the ardent hope that we'll "get it" – that we'll understand and that we'll laugh.

This book is not designed to transform you into a stand-up comic. (Check out the Resources section for books that can help you achieve this goal.) The main focus of this book is to help the average everyday person learn how to attract and create humor in their everyday life.

Developing a stand up routine requires a lot more hard work than most people can imagine. Seinfeld says that it takes him three weeks' worth of work to get five minutes of material. Most comedians say they get one minute of good material a week. What separates comedians from the rest of us is their commitment to capturing a

The next time
someone tells you
they're having a
Déjà Vu,
look at them
with a straight face
and say,
"You told me that
already."

KARYN RUTH WHITE

moment in time, writing it down, crafting it into humor and then adding it to their database of material.

One of the things Karyn Ruth and Jay have noticed is that many comedians say, "Mainly, I do this for me. It just makes my day better and it makes life more interesting." Part of developing your Seventh Sense is about entertaining yourself, and part is about sharing it with others.

When you learn to think like a comedian, you will find yourself in situations that you think are absolutely hilarious (this happens to Karyn Ruth about ten times a day) and the person right next to you has absolutely no idea what you're seeing and finding so funny. They're not seeing the humor at all. Karyn Ruth often asks herself, "Is *anyone else* seeing this or am I working alone here?!" Often you *are* the only one seeing the situation from the humor perspective. That's okay! Think of it as your private little humor moment. Cultivating your Seventh Sense is something you should do for yourself, first and foremost. Then it's not quite as important whether or not someone else gets it.

Don't let terminally serious people squelch your natural joy and spirit. Some people seem to live their lives seeking out misery. CAUTION: they will try to take you with them because misery really does love company. But you have a choice -- you can refuse to go. You can choose to be, stay and live in a good mood.

Karyn Ruth says, "It's important to know how to be funny alone. Humor isn't always about getting a response from other people. The ability to entertain yourself and enjoy your own company is vitally important to your mental health.

"I can be walking around my house and just laughing hysterically at something. And when I laugh, I laugh! You can hear it all over the neighborhood. I'm surprised

At Disney World I overheard a father say to his crying son, "If you don't stop your whining, I'm going to drag your little butt right out of the happiest damn place on earth!"

KARYN RUTH WHITE

my neighbors haven't sent the men in white coats to my door. They really are going to come and get me one of these days. But until they do, I'm going to keep having a good time even if no one else is around to enjoy it with me."

Modeling Comedians

How do comedians see the funny in life? How do they turn on their comedy radar and become aware of the funny stuff around them? And how do they leverage that awareness into comedy and humor?

As a member of the National Speakers Association, Jay found that he was good at improvisational humor, but he wanted to be able to craft specific humor to put in his speeches. That is when he began using Neuro-Linguistic Programming (NLP) techniques to study how comedians run their brains – how they think, how they see life, and how they create consistently deliverable humor.

We can learn how to think, see and be funnier in the same way that most of us learned how to walk and talk: by watching other people do it. All we need is the right set of tools and filters. As a master practitioner of NLP, Jay developed and honed these filters over a decade of study. He then focused this learning on the field of comedy. The simplicity and clarity of what he found surprised him.

Have you ever noticed that comedy is rarely a joke about two guys going into a bar? It's usually best when the joke is universal, about everyday experiences. The comedian shines a spotlight on the crazy, silly, or stupid things we do at work, at home, in relationships, and so on.

Jay found that every comedian uses the same mental process to find and develop humor. Metaphorically, it's a lot like mining:

1. Comedians are always *prospecting* for humor.
2. When they find it, they *mine* it.

Remember when safe sex meant your parents weren't home?

KARYN RUTH WHITE

3. Then they *refine* it.
4. Then they *forge* it into creative jokes, bits, and improvisations that make people laugh.
5. And their *gold* (reward) is laughter.

Comedians, humorists and class clowns notice when something is potentially funny. It's as if they have some sort of comedy radar operating 24/7. It's what we call "cultivating a humor awareness," or being able to *prospect* for potential humor. The pros are able to recognize when there's something funny and turn it into comedy. How do these minds know when there's something funny going on? How do they actually mine and develop humor? How do they take what they find and then sift it into something that's really useful and fun? To better understand the pros, let's first look at your humor style.

Your Humor Style

This book is about learning, developing and leveraging your own personal humor style and material. That's what's fun about comedy – all comedians are different. Think about Gallagher smashing watermelons, Steven Wright's droll delivery, or someone frenetic like Robin Williams. That's what we like, that uniqueness of experience. We invite you to investigate your unique sense of humor by using some of the tools the great comedians use.

One of the first things you should realize is that you already have a style of humor that is a combination of your nature and what you've learned from various people you've seen or known through the years. Humans are masters at learning through detecting patterns of behavior. When you listen to comedians like Mike Myers, David Brenner or Robin Williams talk about their childhoods, invariably one of their parents was funny. And we know

Remember the good old days when you could sneeze and fluid only came out of one end?

KARYN RUTH WHITE

that Robin later studied and modeled Jonathan Winters. Most of us have role models from whom we've learned humor. We call them Humor Heroes. To begin to discover your own humor style, you'll want to delve into your past and remember your own Humor Heroes.

Virtually all comedians also have a humor buddy – someone they can talk to about jokes, ideas, life, etc. So we encourage you to find someone you can work with to share your developing Seventh Sense.

HUMOR HEROES

Exercise:
1. Find a friend to be your humor buddy.
2. In your Seventh Sense Journal, write down at least three people you think are funny (comedians, actors, family members, co-workers, or friends). These should be people whose humor you appreciate and whom you would like to emulate in some way. They can be famous or not. It can be your mother-in-law, your spouse or your weird Uncle Lou.
3. Share with your humor buddy why you really like these people. What it is that you really like about their humor?

JAY'S HUMOR HEROES

"**Robin Williams**. I love the fact that his perspective is so different from the way the average person sees things. I can't imagine spending a lot of time around this level of energy, but as a comedian, I think he is unparalleled. His use of character voices and physical humor are brilliant underscores for his rapid-fire mind. I especially love it when he goes Shakespearean. Many times when dealing with otherwise boring or difficult situations, I will model Robin Williams and this helps lighten the moment.

I found the secret to
looking younger.
Every birthday, I take
one more step back
from the
makeup mirror.
I'm putting my
lipstick on in the
neighbor's yard, now.

KARYN RUTH WHITE

It's hard to take much of anything too seriously when you are viewing it through the eyes of Robin Williams.

"I love **Groucho Marx's** style and lightning wit. I remember watching his classic television show, *You Bet Your Life*, and he asked a man how many children he had. The man replied, 'Eight. I really love kids.' Groucho says, ' Well, I love my cigar too, but I take it out once in a while.' I like going into Groucho mode. When something frustrates me, I'll hunch over and do the cigar move and say, 'This is the most ridiculous thing I've ever seen.'"

"On the other end of the energy spectrum, there's **Steven Wright's** dry, droll delivery and his bizarre perspective on things. Here are a couple of my favorite Steven Wright lines:

'I used to work for a fire hydrant manufacturer. You couldn't park anywhere near the place.'

'I installed a skylight in my apartment. The people above me are furious.'

"His perspective is so original and his observations are so unique. His view of the world coupled with his deadpan, monotone delivery makes for a hilarious effect. Sometimes, in the middle of the day, I'll be doing something and I'll ask myself, *How would Steven Wright see this right now?* Just asking the question makes me laugh.

KARYN RUTH'S HUMOR HEROES

"I have studied **Woody Allen** extensively. I've listened to his album, *Stand-Up Comic,* over 100 times. This album is by far the funniest material I have ever heard. Woody Allen is my idol when it comes to the use of language, his auditory punctuation and his wit. He is by far the best comedy writer I have ever heard. His neurotic character is so well-defined that he can paint a picture quickly and have us laughing madly. 'I'm not afraid of death, I just don't want to be there when it happens.'

I never understand
women who say,
"Sure he's cute, but
he knows it."
What would they
rather have?
An ugly guy
who's just not sure?

KARYN RUTH WHITE

"Here's one of my favorite Woody Allen jokes:

'I don't know if you read it in the paper or not, but my ex-wife was violated. That's how they put it in the New York paper – she was violated. They asked me to comment on it. I said, knowing my ex-wife, it was not a moving violation.'

"Allen is musical in his use of the English language. He also happens to be an accomplished jazz musician. Every word is a note, every story is a verse, and the song itself is hilarious. He will go off on what seem like tangents (like jazz does), and give you punch lines all along the journey to the big payoff.

"Woody Allen's appearance also serves him well as a comedian. He has brilliantly painted himself as the little guy. He's the guy who is overwhelmed and fearful of life and he uses humor as his shield. I think to some extent, we can all relate to that.

"**Paula Poundstone** is absolutely hysterical. Her timing and delivery have an unusual cadence that makes her material even more comical. She can talk for fifteen solid minutes about Pop-Tarts and have you laughing so hard that you're crying. She also does crazy stuff with everyday observations. One of my favorites is a bit she does about parking:

'I live in San Francisco where the parking is impossible. I saw a guy with a sign on his garage that said, *Don't Even Think About Parking Here*. So I sat right there and thought about it. I yelled up at his window, Hey Buddy, I'm thinking about it. Go ahead, call the cops. I'll just tell 'em I was thinking about something else.'

"I love **George Carlin's** use of the English language. I love the way he can take everyday things and make them hilarious. This is a man who made a million dollar routine out of talking about being a class clown. He uses

If you're going to be paid to accomplish nothing, then you better be damn good at it.

QUOTE FROM A FEDERAL EMPLOYEE

his voice brilliantly. He punches his delivery with sound and voice intonation. He is a master at his craft."

CHANNELING YOUR HUMOR HEROES

One of the things we want you to think about is that the people you think are funny probably reflect a part of your own humor style. You may not have as much practice as your Humor Hero, and you certainly won't have as much material, but the fact that their humor resonates with you is a clue about your own humor style. Your Humor Heroes are going to be your coaches as we go through the book. Bring these people to the forefront of your thinking and use them as models and channels as you think about your Seventh Sense.

CHANNELING ROBIN WILLIAMS

Jay's thirteen year old daughter Kelly was having one of those "I'm bored and I hate everyone" kind of days. Jay was having trouble figuring out how to deal with her until he imagined Robin Williams dealing with her. He "tried on" being Robin Williams and suddenly, he found himself channeling Robin Williams. "Imitating his fast-paced delivery, I said, 'Wassup, Mama? You can't be sittin' around all day waitin' to be entertained. This ain't no Sesame Street, Darlin'.'" Kelly gave Jay a strange look and then she laughed and her mood improved.

One of Karyn Ruth's all-time favorite comedians was Paul Lynde. One day she got stopped by a policeman for speeding and she asked herself, *What would Paul Lynde do right now?* So, when the officer came to the window and whipped open the ticket pad and took out a pen, Karyn Ruth stuck her head out the window and said, in a Paul Lynde voice, "I'll have a hamburger and a chocolate shake." She got the ticket, but it was worth the laugh.

If you don't have anything nice to say, come sit next to me.

ALICE R. LONGWORTH

What would one of your Humor Heroes do in a given situation? What goofy things would they say or do? What could they find funny about the moment? How would they make the situation into something funny? For instance, can you picture Robin Williams at an IRS audit?

You can imagine the extreme and see your Humor Hero doing something really off the wall, something you would probably never actually do. Then modify it by asking yourself, "Okay, how can I step out of myself a little here and become a little more like Robin Williams (or whoever your Humor Hero happens to be)?" Find the essence of what it is you like about your Humor Hero and ask yourself how you could be more like that person and still be comfortable with who you are and how you deal with the world. The ability to step into someone else and use their perspective and their coping tools will give you a lot more flexibility in how you respond to life.

HUMOR HERO HOMEWORK

Exercise: In your Seventh Sense Journal:
1. Write about a situation that could benefit from a more humorous perspective.
2. See each of your three Humor Heroes dealing with that situation. Which style would best fit your own style?
3. Now see yourself dealing with that situation as one of your Humor Heroes. Adjust it to fit your own style.
4. Now step into the scene and explore what it would be like to channel this Humor Hero.
5. Step into your future to three or more situations where you could use this new-found ability at work, with family, dating, wherever.

As I've gotten older I only have 70% of my hearing left. But that's O.K.

My doctor gave me a medical ID tag that entitles me to 30% off all of my CDs.

COMEDIAN ELAINE BLAINEY

How long has it been since you've seen or heard your Humor Heroes? Do you actively seek out that wellspring of humor?

Your comedy homework is to rent CDs and videos/DVDs of your favorite Humor Heroes. Rent some movies, tape the sitcoms that you love, record comedians on The Actors Studio and The Comedy Channel. After a really hard day, come home and pop in an hour of your favorite comedy. Your psychological state will improve after watching an hour of comedy. Karyn Ruth has to have an hour of comedy every day. "It doesn't matter how busy I am, I always take my one hour comedy break."

It's all about filling up the laughter well and giving your tired, stressed mind some time to relax and recharge. Actively seek out the people you think are funny. Get some comedy CDs and play them in your car. Make it a weekly ritual to sit down and watch or listen to an hour of your Humor Heroes. Your Seventh Sense will improve by osmosis.

Whenever I hear someone sigh that "Life is hard," I'm always tempted
to ask,
"Compared to what?"

SYDNEY J. HARRIS, JOURNALIST

CHAPTER THREE
HONING YOUR COMEDY RADAR

Carol Burnett said that "comedy is tragedy plus time." The trick is to shorten the distance between the tragedy and the time it takes to see the humor in it. You need to be able to step out and see it a little differently, then come back and find a new perspective about the whole thing. A lot of comedy comes from angst and pain. Think of Woody Allen, who is angst personified and who turns his angst into brilliant comedy.

When you laugh at a problem or situation, just the fact that you are able to laugh means that you've literally pulled yourself out of the moment (at least long enough to laugh at it). When you pull yourself out of the moment, you have a much better opportunity to solve the problem – to see it in a different light and to find a creative solution. Laughter and humor allow you to become an observer of your own life.

This is the key element of comedy awareness. When you become an observer, you have a much better chance of "seeing" the humor.

As Jay was studying comedians, he would hear them say things like, "Well, you have to *pull yourself out* and then you have to *observe yourself* having this experience." George Campbell, a national humorist who does a show about being the world's *worst* motivational speaker, says,

Tragedy is when
I cut my finger.
Comedy is when you
fall into an open
sewer and die.

MEL BROOKS

"To start to understand and develop humor, you have to *take a step back*. You have to *get some distance on it* so that you can see what's going on."

When Jay observed the same train of thought in all of the funny people he talked with, he knew he had found a pattern – a pattern that anyone can learn.

The concept of "stepping back" or "getting outside of yourself" is a consistent pattern among successful comedians. Steven Wright says he feels like the guy standing outside the window looking in at the party.

You may already unconsciously think like this to some degree. Now try it consciously. Say to yourself, "Okay, what would be funny about this if I were on the ceiling looking down at myself in this predicament?" Be willing to entertain a new perspective and take a fresh look at the situation.

Asking the Comedy Questions

The comedians Jay studied all said the same thing: "I ask myself, what's funny about this?" If that fails to generate humor, they ask a different question. "If this were happening to someone else, would it be funny?" National humorist Tim Gard asks himself, "If this were happening to the Lone Ranger, would it be funny?" If this doesn't work, he asks himself, "What is this like?"

Here's an example of how this works: Jay was walking through the Seattle airport and saw a woman standing in a phone booth talking on her cell phone. He thought, *Does she understand the concept of cellular or does she think she has to stand in a phone booth to get her cell phone to work?*

There's a restaurant in the Seattle Airport called "Liar's Seafood." Jay's comedy radar asked, *What's funny*

In an effort to relieve road rage, AAA wants us to flash each other the peace sign.
The good news is, we're halfway there.

KARYN RUTH WHITE

about that name? Then his mind came up with, *Yeah, I'm sure, their fish is fresh!*

There's a store in Phoenix, Arizona called "Guns-R-Us/Postal Plus." It's a gun store and it's also a place where you can mail and ship packages. When Jay saw it he thought, *Isn't that great? You can buy a gun and go postal all in the same store!*

Not everything you come up with is going to be gut-wrenchingly hilarious, but it doesn't matter. The important thing is to start building the neural pathways in your brain and begin training your mind to automatically look for the funny.

One of the things Jay has noticed about his humor style is that he tends to hear humor more easily than he sees it. In NLP terms, he is an auditory learner. He picks up on words like "*Liar's* Seafood." When it comes to visual images, he has a little more trouble making pictures funny. You, too, may be stronger in one sense than another.

Make the choice to turn up the volume a little bit on your senses, including your sense of humor, and say, "I'm going to look and listen. I'm going to put a humor filter on everything I hear and see today."

Some people will think, *Oh, this is ridiculous. I'm not going to do all that work; I have enough things on my mind.* Just start small and watch what happens. It's worth the effort!

Since the beginning
of time,
men have notoriously
been the hunters,
tirelessly
stalking fresh game,
while women have
gathered fruits and
nuts.
Scientists call this
survival of the fittest.
I call it Happy Hour.

KARYN RUTH WHITE

Exercise: Once you've taken a step back from a particular problem or situation, ask yourself the following questions:

1. What's funny about this?
2. If this were happening to someone else, would it be funny?
3. What is this like?

USING YOUR COMEDY RADAR

Sound the alarm: Comedians have an internal alarm that rings, buzzes, clicks, or vibrates when they see, hear, or feel something potentially funny. This feeling is their "trigger" – a sign that there is something worth investigating on their comedy radar.

Take a step back: Getting distance or getting outside of yourself is what psychiatrists call "dissociation" – the ability to get out of your physical body and look back at yourself and your situation from a distance. This is an essential skill for creating comedy. When you can step out of your feelings and get some distance, it is a lot easier to find the funny in any situation, even a tragedy.

Life is too short to dance with ugly men.

OSCAR WILDE

CHAPTER FOUR
FOOL'S GOLD: Mining the Humor

Comedians say, "I'm always finding things that are funny and then writing them down." (Usually in a comedy notebook or captured on a voice-recorder.) They'll scribble down a note about something they thought was funny and then let it sit for a couple of days. Then they bring it back out and look at it in the cold light of reason and ask themselves, "Is this still funny?" Sometimes the answer is no, in terms of material they would present on stage. But through constant analysis and practice, they develop a sense of whether or not their humor will seem funny to others.

Sometimes what seems funny one moment isn't funny the next. Have you ever heard someone say, "Guess you had to be there?" Trying to recreate a funny moment can be difficult to pull off. Sometimes you just have to let it go.

All comedians develop humor by thinking about connections. *What is this like? How does this relate to that? What's the connection between these two things?*

Karyn Ruth saw a woman get into her car, buckle her seat belt and light a cigarette. She asked herself, "What is the connection between those two things? Let's see, the seat-belt prevents death and the cigarette causes it." Her inner comedian said, "Well, here's a woman who can't decide if she's coming or going."

If life is a bowl of cherries, why am I always in the pits?

ERMA BOMBECK

There is irony to be found in human behavior every single day, and irony is humor. Irony is when two opposing messages are being presented as logical, or when an outcome is completely the opposite of what was expected. We say one thing and do another. Turn on your comedy radar and start to ask, "What's ironic about this situation? What's the connection? What's the funny connection?" Sometimes it's just about going with the first thing that comes to your mind and then playing with that word or that idea until you find the funny.

One of the great benefits of having a highly-developed Seventh Sense is that while people around you are stressing out and taking life way too seriously, you have this hilarious movie going on in your head. Even though you may not be verbalizing all that you are thinking, it's helping you better cope with stress, mentally, emotionally and physiologically.

Jay was working with a business team a few years ago. It was the very first day and they were trying to get started, but everybody was mad about having been yanked away from home and sent to Salt Lake City for two months to work on a project. No one was having a good day, including Jay. The class had been going on for about two hours and things were getting more and more stressful. Then one guy said, "I think we need a reality break." What he meant to say was a "reality check." Some part of Jay's brain tried to imagine what a reality break would look like, and then he went into weird, spastic contortions. The whole team stopped and stared at him. Jay looked back at them and said, "You told me to take a reality break and I did," and they all laughed hysterically. It was a good five minute laugh, and from that point on the team was able to be productive.

The pen is mightier than the sword, and considerably easier to write with.

MARTY FELDMAN

Humor is a risk, but it holds magical possibilities. Jay's willingness to act crazy cut through all the tension and helped the team relax. What they were probably thinking was, "We better get this project done as quickly as possible, because this guy could blow at any moment." Jay took the humor risk because he knew the situation couldn't get any worse. The team was going down hill and they still had two months ahead of them. Jay's one episode of wild, physical humor set a lighter tone for the next two months. Now that's magic!

For those of you who are thinking, *Yeah that's great but I could/would never do that,* we believe there is a moment when you wonder, *Should I take the humor path or not?* More often than not, the more you take the humor path, the more comfortable you'll become risking humor.

It's healthy to have that voice in your head that says, "Okay, I have this thought. Here's the situation. Is it appropriate for me to do this right now?" Jay went through that process before deciding to go wild in front of his class because he knew he had to try something. Trust your instincts to tell you whether using humor is appropriate and worth the risk.

Karyn Ruth was presenting a humor program to a group of Funeral Directors. It was an early morning program and the audience wasn't laughing. She tried her best stuff on them and got no response, and she still had another hour to go. She started to panic. A small bead of perspiration started running down her back. The little voice in her head was screaming, "This is not a drill! These people are not playing along. Do something! Do something now!" So she told herself, "Okay, Karyn Ruth, you can continue on and just try to get through this, or you can name the game. You can risk stepping out of your program and find out what's going on here." That's what she

A fool and his money are soon elected.

WILL ROGERS

did. She stopped in the middle of her program and said, "Okay, now I *know* I'm funny. This is funny stuff I'm doing up here, but you're not laughing. No one in the room is making a sound. I don't understand it, because at first glance you all looked so lifelike." There was "dead" silence in the room ... and then uproarious laughter. (Thank God!) It turns out they weren't laughing because they didn't think it was appropriate in their line of work. They then proceeded to spend a lively hour talking about the use of humor in the funeral business, and when it's appropriate and helpful and when it isn't. (By the way, they invited her back the following year.)

Karyn Ruth knew stepping out of her program was a big risk, but she knew she had to do something. Taking the risk saved her program. Unfortunately, however, there are no guarantees; that's why they call it a risk. It could also have gone the other way. But, she was playful in her delivery, not mean, and she thinks that made all the difference.

PLAYING WITH WORDS

Having fun with the English language is a big part of creating comedy. Listening with a comedian's ear to how certain words are used, the context of their usage, their double meanings, etc., is a great step toward developing your Seventh Sense.

Here is an example of a comedy bit Karyn Ruth wrote playing with the double meaning of the word "filly:"

"In every state in the Union except Texas, I'm considered a grown female adult. But when I hit Texas soil, I suddenly become a filly. 'Well, hi there, Darlin', aren't you a fine lookin' filly? How long y'all gonna be in town?' I just stomp my foot three times and run before they try to check my teeth."

I went abroad and came back the same way.

MAE WEST

POINT OF VIEW

Comedians are masters at changing their point of view to find the funny. We looked at how comedians can step out of any situation, good or bad, into an observer position where they can ask, "What's funny about this?" From this perspective, you can shift into almost any other point of view. For instance, you can step into animate or inanimate objects and notice what's funny from that other perspective.

Comedians are not the only people who change their point of view. Jay read a book by Dr. Jonas Salk, the inventor of the polio vaccine, in which he talks about changing perspectives. "Well first, I tried on what it was like to be a virus and infect a cell, then I tried on what it was like to be the immune system dealing with that infected cell." As he was experimenting, he was trying on (modeling) these other realities to get another perspective before taking his hypotheses to the lab and testing them. That's how he came up with the vaccine for polio!

Comedians use this same questioning technique to create humor. They're like scientists of humor, constantly experimenting with questions like, *What is this like? What's funny here? Why does this interest me? Where is the comedy in this?* So if you want to develop your Seventh Sense, try on various perspectives and points of view and ask as many questions as you can. Try thinking from a dog's point of view, or your cat's, or maybe even that of your goldfish. For example, here's a bit written from the goldfish perspective:

"Ever think about what goes on in a goldfish bowl? Two goldfish stuck together in this tiny little bowl. Passing each other hundreds of times a day. Every morning, every

Outside of the killings, Washington has one of the lowest crime rates in the country.

MAYOR MARION BARRY, WASHINGTON, DC.

afternoon, all day long, passing each other, 'Hi Bill. Hi Frank. Hi Bill. Hi Frank. Hi Bill. Hi Frank.' Reminds me of the office."

Paula Poundstone is a master of the use of perspective. She takes the world and twists it 180 degrees. Here is an example of her use of perspective:

"I don't really understand children. I try to put them down for a nap and they cry. I don't understand this. As an adult, can you remember the last time you didn't want to sleep? Just once I'd like to see a child come up to me and say, 'I'm beat! I've been at the Leggos for an hour and a half, the Big Wheel's jackknifed at the end of the driveway. I'm just going to go into the back room and lie down.' I'd say, 'My, how mature. You go ahead. I'll hold your calls.'"

Here's another classic Poundstone perspective:

"When my cats do something wrong, as a punishment, I squirt them with a water gun. The other day I was taking a shower and I caught my three cats staring at me through the glass thinking, 'Wow, she must have done something really, really bad.'"

Seeing everyday life from the perspective of your cat or dog is hilarious. Or, you can "try on" being your boss, or your client, or your spouse, or even your mother-in-law. Seeing life from another person's point of view opens the door, not only for humor, but for compassion, understanding and empathy.

I dated a man who
lied so often
he started every story
with
"Once Upon A Time."

COMEDIAN MARY ELLEN RINALDI

CHAPTER FIVE
TURNING CRAP INTO GOLD

The first draft of anything is crap.
Hemingway

We love this quote by Hemingway. We love the fact that he used the word crap. Another great quote on the subject of first writing attempts comes from Natalie Goldberg, author of *Writing Down The Bones*. Natalie says, "Writing is making a mess and cleaning it up." Like the panhandlers of the gold rush days, you have to spend a lot of time sifting through the raw material before you find the comedy gold. The sifting and refining process is where a lot of people get frustrated because, let's face it, it takes a lot of patience to squat by the river for hours on end looking for a nugget of value.

First, let's look at your raw material, your "crap," as Hemingway would say. What are you starting with?

There is great temptation to use humor from the Internet or "borrowed humor" from somewhere else as the easiest and fastest route to assembling raw material. A word of caution here: when you tell a joke you've heard somewhere else, there's a good chance that your listener will have heard it, too. But when your humor is based on your own experience, the odds are very slim that anyone will have heard the story before. Using your *own* life

It isn't pollution
that's harming the
environment. It's the
impurities in our
air and water
that are doing it.

DAN QUAYLE

experiences, beliefs and attitudes as fodder for great comedy will distinguish your humor as original. Telling a funny story about your daughter's first driving lesson or your middle-aged spouse's foray into being a first-time college student will ring true and feel a lot more authentic than if you start with, "Two guys walk into a bar…"

Formula jokes have a tendency to make you sound like a "hack." Hack is the term used in the stand-up comedy world for a person who isn't very original. Karyn Ruth knows a hairdresser whose idea of making it on the comedy stage is taking jokes from the Internet and tweaking them to make them his own. She suggested to him that he use the abundant supply of humor he finds all around him in a hair salon. See the difference?

So start looking at your life as a playground for humor. We know what you're thinking: *But my life is boring, normal, unexciting. What could I possibly find funny in my own life? Even if I did find something funny, who would want to hear about it?* Go back and study your Humor Heroes. Don't they talk about their lives? You can do the same thing. The ordinary, everyday stuff is hilarious. Seinfeld had a hit show about nothing!

THE STRUCTURE OF A JOKE

Jokes have a simple structure:

setup –> punch line –> punch word

The **setup** gets the audience's mind moving in one direction by painting a picture. The **punch line** flips the momentum in a new direction, which makes us laugh. Many jokes are written so that the last word, the **punch word**, flips the picture created in the audience's mind.

You know road rage
is a problem when
the bumper sticker
on the truck in front
of you says,
"Cover Me,
I'm Changing Lanes."

KARYN RUTH WHITE

CRAFTING A JOKE

So how do you start to find the nuggets of gold in your pile of crap? Or put another way, how do you start to craft jokes from your everyday observations?

Get out your comedy pan, we're going to start sifting. Look at your raw material and start sifting through it using the following questions:

- What's funny about this?
- If this were happening to someone else, would it be funny?
- What is this like? What other things come to mind in association with this?
- How do I feel about it?
- What's my attitude about this? Mad? Amazed? Confused?
- Why do I think it's funny?
- Is this a universal concept?
- Where is the tension in this story?
- Who are the characters?
- How can I bring the characters to life with my facial expressions, body posture, gestures and voice?

This is a partial list to get you started. It's really amusing when workshop students come back whining, "But this is hard! I thought comedy was supposed to be fun!" The sifting process is tedious and requires patience. If it were easy, everyone would be a stand-up comedian! The reward is amazing, though, for those who can learn this step. If you can get through this step, you can write a decent joke. And if you can write a decent joke, you can probably learn to write a great joke, and then you can write another one. Before long you can string a few of

Whoever said money can't buy happiness, didn't know where to shop.

UNKNOWN

these great jokes together to make a great story. Then you can practice and learn how to tell that great story consistently so that it gets a great laugh every time and, well, life don't get much better than that! So hunker down and let's start sifting.

ASSOCIATIONS

A technique for wiring your brain to think how comedians think is an exercise called "Associations." As a stand-up, when you're trying to come up with material, when you're staring at a blank piece of paper, making a list of associations and looking for connections is a great place to start.

By looking for new associations, your brain starts to build new neural pathways and you start to connect things that you would never have connected before. You start to answer the question, "What is this like?"

You begin to see things in different ways and that's all humor is. Remember? New perspective. If there is a situation that the rest of the world is looking at one way, the comedian steps outside of the situation, stands in a different spot, so to speak, and presents it to you in a totally different way. How many times have you heard a comedian deliver a brilliant line and think, *Why didn't I ever notice that?*

Gallagher has a wonderful line: "If 7-Eleven is open 24 hours a day, then why is there a lock on the door?" How many times have you gone into a 7-Eleven? Have you never noticed the lock? Comedians notice these kinds of details every day. So can you. You can begin to see these things if you are willing to constantly ask, "What's funny/ironic/weird about this?"

ASSOCIATIONS

WOMEN	CARS
Bad Drivers	Sports
Bodies	Bodies
Fast Women	Fast Cars
Model	Model
High Maintenance	Expensive
Beautiful	Luxury
Topless	Convertible
High Beams	High Beams
Makeover	Rear End
In the Shop	Bumpers
	Engine
	Motor
	Overhaul
	Exotic
	Imports/Domestic
	Four on the Floor

Possible jokes:

Women are like cars because...
#1: They're always in the shop.
#2: If you want a high-performance model, expect high
     maintenance.
#3: They can blind you with their high beams.

Now let's get a little more creative:
"My wife causes quite a commotion when she drives our
'64 Ford Mustang, top down, through the neighborhood. I'm just glad we didn't get the convertible."

Associations can create connections between two seemingly unrelated categories: e.g., women and cars, cigarette smoking and electricity, politics and honesty.

Exercise: In your Seventh Sense Journal, choose two words, preferably nouns, like Cars and Women. (See example on the opposite page.)

1. Jump-start your mind by simply listing all of the words you can think of about these two nouns.
2. Look at the two lists for similarities between any of the words. Look for words that could be used to describe both subjects in some way. Look for the humor potential in the relationships between all of the words and start creating humor. Just let the ideas flow; don't edit yourself at this point. Remember, writing is making a mess and cleaning it up.
3. Now, write some jokes. Think, *How can I connect these two totally separate topics in a funny way? What do these two things have in common? How am I going to put these two things together?*

REAL LIFE EXAMPLE

Following is an example from a bit Karyn Ruth uses in her stand-up act. We're inserting the word "laugh" where the audience always laughs to help give you a feel for the pacing.

"I recently quit smoking. (applause) Thank you. I've quit smoking, six, seven, eighteen times so far, (laugh) so it's not like I can't do it. (laugh) It's gotten to where you can't smoke anywhere anymore. I went to a restaurant in California. I asked for Smoking. They sat me in Montana. (laugh) I finally went to one of those clinics where they help you stop smoking, you know the kind, where they give you a shock every time you take a drag of a cigarette.

I recently went to a clinic to quit smoking. They gave me a shock every time I took a drag of a cigarette. It was supposed to stop me from smoking. It backfired. Now I have two addictions. Nicotine *and* electricity. Now after dinner, I light up and *then* I have a cigarette.

KARYN RUTH WHITE

(laugh) Take a drag, get a shock. Take a drag, get a shock. (laugh) This was supposed to stop me from smoking. It backfired. (pause) Now I have two addictions. Nicotine *and* electricity. Now after dinner, I light up and *then* I have a cigarette."

Let's dissect just the last line of this bit: "Now after dinner, I light up and *then* I have a cigarette."

The two subjects are Smoking and Electricity. Karyn Ruth got the idea for this bit when she lived in California when shock-aversion nonsmoking clinics were first coming out. She didn't really go to one of these clinics, but the key is that the concept is real; these places really exist. So she used poetic license and wrote the story from a personal perspective, which makes it even funnier because the audience can now relate to the story on a personal level.

To get to her payoff, or final punch line, she started listing her word associations. She asked herself the sifting questions: "What's this like? What are the associations that come to mind when I think of smoking and electricity together?" She got out a piece of paper and put the heading SMOKING on one side of the page and ELECTRICITY on the other side. Then she started listing the words that came to mind under each of those headings. She wasn't trying to find humor yet; she was just brainstorming associations.

"Sometimes, I'll start a list and then just put it on my bedside table and keep adding words over the next few days as they come to me. Or, I'll be watching TV and something will remind me of another word and I'll keep listing words until I have about twenty on each side."

Obviously, the more words you can come up with, the better, but if you can come up with a minimum of ten, then chances are good you'll be able to get something funny.

KARYN RUTH'S LIST

SMOKING
Cigarettes
Nicotine
Filters
Tar
Ultra Light
Lungs
Cancer
The Patch
Nicoderm CQ
Clinics
Shock Treatments
Hypnosis
Brown Teeth
Coughing
Smell
Marlboro Man
Advertising
Old Movies
Bogart
Lighting Up
Bum a butt
Virginia Slims
Camel Reds
Cowboys
Bars
Comedy Clubs

ELECTRICITY
Wattage
Fuse
Light
Candle
Shock
Outlet
Ohms
Wiring
Electrician
Expensive
Babyproofing Outlets
Positive and Negative
Charges
Jump-Starting
Black Out
Light Bulb
Lamp
Lampshade
Disconnect
Bad Wiring
Fire
Shortage

The important thing to remember here is not to edit yourself. Just free associate – nothing is stupid, write it all down. You'll notice that each of Karyn Ruth's lists has a little over twenty words. Once she has the two lists, she takes a look at them and uses her sifting questions: "How are these two subjects alike? Are there any common words or themes that I might be able to play with? Let's see, Light up – Light, Shock Treatment – Shock. Okay, now I have two possibilities and I can start to write a joke."

The following is the running mental dialogue of the comedy writing thought process it took to get to her punch line:

"Okay, to light up – what does that mean? To have a cigarette – it can also mean to light up a room – there's a double meaning here that might be a possible joke. Okay, the joke is ... that after dinner (which is the time people most enjoy a cigarette so smokers and nonsmokers alike will understand that) I want both a cigarette and some form of electricity because I have established that I have two addictions – nicotine and electricity. Now after dinner, I'm looking for a cigarette and a cattle prod – no, that's not quite it. What else is like a cattle prod that involves electricity? A stun gun? An open outlet? Now after dinner, I'm looking for a cigarette and a live outlet. No, that's not it either. Now after dinner, I'm looking for a cigarette and a stun gun. Okay, funnier – funny visual image – but I think there's a better line. I'd really like to write something a little more clever – something that plays on the double meaning of light. Now after dinner, I light up – hey wait a minute, that can mean both things; it can mean that I light up as in having a cigarette and it can also mean that I light up as in being electrically charged – hey I'm on to something here – now how do I say it funny? I could reverse the order; instead of having a cigarette and

LAUNDROMAT
Suds
Dirty Laundry
Wash
Rinse
Soak
Coin Operated
Hangers
Quarters
Detergent
Stuffed Shirt
Bleach
Fluff and Fold
Tumble
Agitate
Softener
Quick Wash
Load
Creeps
Crying Children
Dirty
Noisy
Basket

DATING
First Date
Blind Date
Internet Dating
Score
Roll in the Hay
Casual Sex
Classified Ads
Match.com
Small Talk
Nervous
Rejection
Losers
Disappointment
Excitement
Fun
Embarrassment
Weirdos
Swingin' Single
Playboy
User
Taker

then looking for electricity, why don't I make it sound like I'm talking about having a cigarette when I say, Now after dinner, I light up...(then I'll pause, letting the audience form the visual of me having a cigarette and then the joke will be the surprise ending)...and *then* I have a cigarette. So the line goes, 'Now after dinner, I light up (pause) and *then* I have a cigarette.' That's it! That's the joke!"

Karyn Ruth got so excited when she finally came up with this line. She had been doing this bit with the Cattle Prod or Stun Gun ending for a while and it just never landed the kind of laugh she wanted. She knew she had to come up with a different ending. The process just described took over two hours and a lot of brain work. Two hours! But the first time she delivered it and it got a huge laugh, that two hour investment paid off. And every time she tells it now, it consistently gets a great laugh. So, was that two hours worth the effort? You betcha! And you can do this too!

Here is another example of using word associations to build a joke. This took place in one of the Seventh Sense Workshops. Jay and Karyn Ruth asked the class as a whole to pick two random subjects and then challenged them to write a joke in fifteen minutes using the free association process just described. The two subjects were Dating and Laundromat. The class started by listing all of the words they could think of under the two headings, and came up with the lists shown on the opposite page.

Look at these two lists and start to go through them, looking for word connections. From these lists, circle whatever words you think you could use in a joke about Dating and the Laundromat. Some of the connecting words our class came up with were shirt, agitate, and tumble. They picked "shirt" because it can be used in the phrase "stuffed shirt," which could describe a date. They picked "tumble"

You know you've reached middle age when you're no longer laughing at the Craftmatic Adjustable Bed commercials.

KARYN RUTH WHITE

because of its double-meaning – tumble dry and Hey Baby, wanna tumble? They picked "agitate" because it can be used several ways – it's a setting on a washer and a verb to describe someone's mood.

Then we brainstormed jokes as a class. Bear in mind, they weren't all winners, but we kept trying until we got one we thought was good. Here are some of the jokes the class came up with from the two lists:

Joke #1: I met a guy in a Laundromat. He turned out to be a real stuffed shirt. On the first date, I got so agitated when he asked me to tumble.

Joke #2: Dating is like going to the Laundromat. It's coin operated. It's a quick spin. And you never have enough change.

Joke #3: Dating is like going to the Laundromat. You go through a lot of agitation for a quick tumble and then you end up doing it yourself.

The class came up with three jokes in fifteen minutes. Which one would you choose as the best? Here is our take on them:

Joke #1: Cute but corny. It uses too many double-entendres. Joke #2: Not bad, but not hilarious. Joke #3: Really good, funny, and clever.

The punch line, "end up doing it yourself," we felt was funny and clever enough not to be offensive.

UNCONSCIOUS COMPETENCE

Remember the first time you tried to drive a car or ride a bike? It required a lot of conscious effort, didn't it? And even if you haven't ridden a bicycle in years, you can probably still ride one. The same is true of comedy; once

Everything is funny as long as it is happening to somebody else.

WILL ROGERS

you learn how to craft jokes and practice, it will begin to become automatic.

Jay still remembers the first time this happened for him. He was watching the TV show, *Ally McBeal*. If you remember, the star of the show, Calista Flockhart, was extremely thin. Then one day Jay was reading an article about how mice on a reduced-calorie diet live up to twice as long as mice that can eat as much as they want. This joke automatically formed in his mind:

"Scientists have found that mice on a reduced-calorie diet live up to twice as long as mice that eat whatever they want. **(setup)** If this works for people, then Calista Flockhart should live for a *millennium.*" **(punch line, punch word)**

Now, maybe it's not the best joke ever written, but it came out fully formed without thinking about it. That's when Jay knew he had succeeded in integrating the joke writing process into his mental software.

Exercise: In your Seventh Sense Journal:
1. Write down two categories that you want to write a joke about: e.g., Husbands and Power Tools, Girlfriends and Sports Cars, Dieting and Work.
2. Generate a list of twenty words that you associate with each category.
3. Compare the two lists. What's funny?
4. Craft a joke with a **setup**, **punch line** and **punch word**.

The first few times it's hard because it's unfamiliar. But as you continue to write, it will get easier. Then, it's only a matter of time and repetition before it becomes natural.

My thighs are the only things in the office that haven't been downsized.

KARYN RUTH WHITE

CHAPTER SIX
REFINING THE RUBBLE

Congratulations, you're down to a better grade of crap. You have a few good ideas for jokes, now what? Now it's time to pick through what's left of the rubble and refine it in your continued search for comedy gold. In this chapter we'll touch on some of the techniques for honing existing joke ideas. This is not meant to be a comprehensive guide on comedy writing, but even if you don't plan to write jokes, knowing how the process works can be a useful step toward enhancing your Seventh Sense.

Comedians go through a tedious editing process to mine and refine their material. After hours of crafting, honing and practicing, they will have a joke that gets a laugh every time and sounds very natural. If you are interested in becoming a serious student of comedy writing, check out the Resources section at the back of the book for our suggestions for further study.

FROM PANHANDLER TO PENHANDLER

There's never anything extra in a well-written joke — no extra words, no extra ideas, nothing but the essential information to support the punch line. Henny Youngman's "Take my wife, please," is possibly the best example of a tightly-written joke. Every word must serve the ultimate

I've been on a diet for
two weeks and
all I've lost is
two weeks.

TOTIE FIELDS

purpose of the joke. If its inclusion isn't critical to the success of the joke, it must be eliminated. This is the art of editing. Any word that doesn't pull its own weight needs to be cut.

Karyn Ruth will tell you from her comedy writing experience that there is nothing more thrilling than getting a joke as "clean and tight" as it can possibly get. Clean and tight are two words used in comedy writing to mean, written as clearly and as succinctly as possible.

For example, Henny Youngman would never deliver his joke like this: "Hey, would one of you guys take my wife, pretty please?" It changes the whole meaning of the joke. "Take my wife" is originally interpreted by the listener to mean "Take my wife, for instance..." then the **punch line** or **punch word**, in this case, makes us laugh because we now realize he is begging us to literally take his wife. See how a few seemingly harmless extra words can change the entire rhythm and meaning of the joke?

Let's look at our joke from the previous chapter.

Premise: Dating is like going to the Laundromat.

Setup: There's a lot of agitation for a quick tumble...

Punch line: and then you end up doing it yourself.

Notice that we didn't say:

Premise: *Sometimes I think that* dating is like going to the *local* laundromat *to do your laundry.*

Setup: *You end up having to go through* a lot of agitation *just to get* a quick tumble.

Punch line: And then *after all that,* you end up doing it yourself.

In the second example, there are 22 extra words. The italicized words are nonessential.

You know you've been single too long when you're getting dressed up to go to Home Depot.

KARYN RUTH WHITE

GET SPECIFIC

Comedy loves specificity. It's not a car, it's a Ford. It's not a Ford, it's a Mustang. It's not a Mustang, it's a '64 Mustang. The more specific you are, the easier it will be for your audience to form a mental picture. People are more likely to get involved with your setups and stories when you give them specific information.

We've told you to get specific, but we also need to say that the audience doesn't want everything spelled out for them. Audiences want signposts of specifics and then they want you to leave them a little room to fill in their own picture.

The old radio shows did this beautifully. They painted a vivid picture while letting the listeners fill in some of their own details. Have you ever been to the movie adaptation of a book you've read and been disappointed by the way the characters looked or sounded? This is because the author did such a good job with character development that you were given the essential information about the character and allowed to fill in your own details. This is what a good joke does.

JOKE STRUCTURE

When most of us think of a joke, we think in terms of a standard, overused format: "Two guys walk into a bar..." or "A priest and a rabbi..."

When a comedian thinks about writing a joke, he or she is more interested in writing about something personal, something from real life or current events. Great humor is timeless and it deals with subjects that are timeless. Think about the *I Love Lucy Show* or *The Honeymooners*, or the television sitcom *Everybody Loves*

Why won't southern women go to orgies? They just can't bear the thought of writing all those thank you notes.

SOUTHERN GAL LINDA JENNINGS

Raymond. These are people dealing with real-life, everyday situations in a hilarious way. If you want your humor to have wide appeal and a long shelf-life, then get real! Create jokes about those universal experiences we've all had and from which we all need some relief.

Remember the word association exercise we did earlier? Now you can refine ideas into the standard joke format: **setup –> punch line –> punch word**.

Setup

A good setup does just that – it sets up the picture or story; it seduces the audience into listening. The listener thinks you're taking them in one direction and then the laugh comes when you surprise them by taking them in a totally different direction. For example, here's a setup: "I don't shoplift." Here's the punch line/punch word: "Anymore." Another example – setup: "Take my wife." The punch line/punch word: "Please." Think about the mental image you got just from the setup and then think about why you laughed at the punch line.

Here's a longer example, a joke Karyn Ruth wrote about real-life:

"People know me as a comedian, but I'm also an accomplished fiction writer. I recently finished a beautiful piece of fiction. I call it My Federal Tax Return. The IRS suggested that I call the sequel, Audit."

There are three setups in this joke:

Setup #1: People know me as a comedian, but I'm also an accomplished fiction writer.

Setup #2: I recently finished a beautiful piece of fiction that I'm very proud of.

Punch line #1: I call it My Federal Tax Return.

Setup #3: The IRS suggested that I call the sequel,

Punch line/word #2: Audit.

TOP TEN WAYS YOU KNOW YOUR JUGGLING IS IMPROVING

10. Your cuts have healed.

9. You're no longer a threat to the audience.

8. You're no longer a threat to yourself.

7. The cats stay in the room when the props come out.

6. One hand knows what the other hand's doing.

5. Your hair has grown back after the torch trick.

4. Your costume is no longer made of asbestos.

3. Your balls are not your mortal enemies.

2. You no longer say 1, 2, 3, Crap!

1. When they yell Oooooh and Aaah, not "Oh My GOD!"

A good setup makes the listeners believe they know where you're going with the joke, and then the punch line shatters that picture and replaces it with something totally unexpected. A good setup "sets up" the listeners' expectations; a good punch line proves them wrong.

The best setup is a relatively short one. A common comedy rule is, the longer the setup, the funnier the joke has to be. The listener doesn't want to sit through a long setup for a mediocre joke. Judy Carter, in her excellent book, *Stand-Up Comedy*, says that "the attention span of an average drinking audience is one to four lines." So challenge yourself to write your joke with a maximum of four lines.

If you would like a detailed look at joke writing and joke structure, we highly recommend Judy Carter's books. (See Resources section.)

If you're studying to be a stand-up comic, you will need to discipline yourself to start looking for what's funny and then craft it into material that will make people laugh. Like any new endeavor, be it golf, skiing, or adding numbers in your head, the more you practice it, the sooner it will become second nature. Your initial learning curve may be a little tough, but the payoff will be worth it.

So ... What's The Joke?

This book is designed as a springboard to help you develop your unique humor style. A major part of understanding humor is understanding how a joke is built. Believe it or not, professional comedians feel lucky if they get one minute of new material a week. Even a minute a week of new comedy is pretty amazing when you look at the time and effort they put into it. Jerry Seinfeld says it takes him three weeks to get five minutes of solid material (material he knows will get a laugh every time.)

Take my wife.
Please!

HENNY YOUNGMAN

So, as you begin to write your own jokes, remember that this is not something that comes naturally even to the people you think are comedy geniuses. They have to work at it and so will you. But writing a good joke is something you can train yourself to do and the payoffs are worth the effort.

YOU MIGHT BE A REDNECK IF...

One common comedy format that Jeff Foxworthy has used brilliantly is, "You might be a _____, if_____." You can use this format or a variation of it to jump-start your humor. "You might be a redneck, if you introduce someone to your wife and your sister and there's only one woman standing next to you." - Jeff Foxworthy

EXAGGERATE

Exaggeration is funny. "Your mother's so fat, when she sits around the house, she sits *around the house*." Or the classic, "You're so ugly, when you were born they slapped your mother." You get the idea. If you can exaggerate a quality, it's funny. Here's a joke Karyn Ruth wrote using this concept:

"My mother is the slowest human being on earth. I've never seen her hurry for anything. My father calls her 'Lightning.' One day I was waiting for a bus and I looked down to see a snail stick his head out of his shell. There I was, this big human, looking straight into the eyes of a tiny snail. I said, 'Whatcha doin', little fella?' He said, 'I'm waiting for your mom.'"

TOP TEN LISTS

One of the most common formats for creating comedy is the Top Ten List. David Letterman has made the Top Ten List a household name, and his lists are published in

I recently finished a beautiful piece of fiction. It's called,

"My Federal Tax Return."

The IRS suggested I call the sequel, "Audit."

KARYN RUTH WHITE

many major newspapers. Cut them out or copy them and put them in your Seventh Sense Journal for reference.

Here's a top ten list for you to complete. The top ten ways you know you're getting funnier are:

10. The spontaneous vomiting has stopped.
9. People are avoiding you less at parties.
8. People will actually look you in the eyes.
7. They really are laughing with you, not at you.
6. You're eating tomatoes, not dodging them.
5. _____
4. _____
3. _____
2. _____
1. _____

SO, WHERE YA FROM?

Another comedy format is the geographical format. For instance, "You know you're from Colorado when you think there are only three seasons: Broncos, Elk and Skiing." Comedians often use this format to write jokes about the city in which they are performing.

I think these
teenagers who pierce
their noses are
very smart.
When they get old,
they'll have the
perfect place to hook
their oxygen tube.

COMEDIAN ELAINE BLAINEY

JUMP-START YOUR CREATIVITY

When you're stuck...

- Start with an association exercise. (See Chapter 5)

- Try on the persona of one of your Humor Heroes. (See Chapter 2) Imagine writing or telling the joke like they would.

- Start with a common format.

  He's so _____, he's _____.

  You might be a _____, if_____.

  You know you're from _____, when_____.

POLISHING YOUR NUGGETS

Now that you've written a few jokes, practice adding a little dimension to them. Comedians call this, "polishing your material."

You can bring life to your lines in many ways. You can enhance your delivery with a simple gesture or a slight change in voice inflection. You can use props to underscore your meaning. You can deliver your material as a certain character, or you can change the meaning of the material completely just by saying it with a certain attitude.

GIVE ME SOME ATTITUDE

Every comedian approaches a piece of material with a specific attitude. Think about some of your favorites. Remember Jackie Gleason as Ralph Cramden? What was his prevailing attitude? How was it different than the attitude of his sidekick, Ed Norton, played by the late,

Whenever my grandfather would get a wedgie, he'd say, "I think I've got a letter in my mailbox."

KARYN RUTH WHITE

great Art Carney? How about the comedy of Woody Allen? What prevailing attitude does he portray? Or Lucille Ball; what was her attitude? Think about your Humor Heroes and observe their comedy styles and prevailing attitudes when they tell jokes. What attitude would work most effectively with your material?

You can always change your attitude based on the topic you're discussing. For instance, you can be angry when you're talking about traffic, worried when you're talking about the IRS, frustrated when you're talking about dating, etc. When you bring a specific attitude to your material, you are giving the listener a specific point of view, a specific perspective on something.

Try rehearsing the same material over and over while trying on different attitudes. Try a least three different attitudes, i.e., angry, bewildered, amused. See which one feels the funniest, truest, or most effective to you. Which one works best with your topic? Try rehearsing with your humor buddy and see what response you get. The beauty of delivering your material with attitude is that you can present the same material in different ways and give it totally different meanings. By experimenting with different attitudes, you can determine which attitude gives you the response you're looking for.

PUNCHING A WORD

Another polishing technique is to practice your material to see how the meaning changes according to which word you emphasize. Putting emphasis on a certain word in comedy is called "punching" a word.

Example: "What do Valley Girls sing around the campfire? Kum–bye-YAAAHHH!" Putting the emphasis on YAH and stretching it out to sound like a valley girl makes this a funny joke. Example: say the following line like an

I left my last job
because I was
involved in five sexual
harassment suits.
I'm not worried.
I don't think they can
prove anything.

KARYN RUTH WHITE

adult would say it. "I am so over it." Now say it like a 16 year old girl would say it. Which word did you punch the first time? Probably "over." The second time? Probably "so." Remember how Chandler Bing talked on Friends? Which word would he punch in the following line? "Could you be any more weird?" That's right, "be."

We all have a unique and natural rhythm to our speech. Start to notice how you communicate with other people and play around with how you might change your inflection or your attitude or your word emphasis to get a different response.

CHARACTERIZATION

One way to animate your material is to deliver it in the voices and gestures of particular characters. This is called "characterization." Women and men do it all the time. When you hear women talk to other women about the men in their lives, they'll say, "I told my husband for the hundredth time to mow the lawn and he says, (then they'll shift into a whining man's voice) 'Ah, come on Honey, the game's on.'" And when men talk to each other about the women in their lives, they say, "I'm sitting there watching the game and she's screaming, (in a shricking woman's voice) 'You need to mow the damn lawn!'"

We all innately know how to shift into characterization. Now practice it with your material. Sometimes it's easier to be funny when you can be a character, when you're somebody other than yourself. So what other voice or character tones could you use? How would your material sound delivered in your impression of your mother's voice, your mother in-law's, your weird Uncle Lou's or a famous actor's? How would your material sound delivered as Columbo, Bogart or Mae West? Use your imagination. The great thing about using characterization is that it

Words of Wisdom from Children

If you want a kitten, start out by asking for a horse. Naomi, age 15

Never trust a dog to watch your food. Patrick, 10

When your mom is mad at your dad, don't let her brush your hair. Taylia, 11

Never tell your mom her diet's not working. Michael, 14

Never try to baptize a cat. Eileen, 8

COMPILED BY VALERIE MASS

adds flavor and variety to the tone and rhythm of your material.

Start to notice the gestures and expressions of people in your everyday life. Ask yourself, "How would I impersonate this person?" Then practice bringing a character to life with gestures, tone of voice, posture, facial expression, etc.

Here's a friendly note of caution: If you do impressions of famous people, make sure you do a good impression. The same advice goes for people who want to use different dialects in their act or presentation. Try it out on your humor buddy first, before performing it on stage.

Not only is life a bitch, it has puppies.

ADRIENNE GUSOFF

CHAPTER SEVEN
BEFORE YOU GO PUBLIC

Life is a risk. Humor is a risk. Hell, backing out of your driveway is a risk! While using humor can be risky, whether in a stand-up routine or in a business presentation, there are ways to minimize that risk.

GET A SECOND OPINION

Unless you have professionally, and successfully, been using humor publicly for several years and trust your own instincts, it is always a good idea to test a new line on a trusted source, like a humor buddy, to get feedback. You can also try slipping a line into a conversation and notice what type of reaction it gets. If people laugh, that's a good sign; if they look at you in stunned silence, you might not be ready to go public.

One of the hardest things to do is to accept less than positive feedback from people without taking it personally. Especially if you've worked really hard on a bit and then someone you trust (like your spouse or your humor buddy) is telling you they don't think it's funny. The temptation is to start to doubt the person you tested it on. You start thinking things like, *How much do I really like this person anyway?* Try to resist this urge. After all, isn't it better to bomb in front of one person than in front of

When I was a kid I had huge feet. The first time I went into a shoe store they measured my feet on that silver scale. The scale was the only thing in the store that fit me. Bought two of them. Wore them home. Told my friends they were Birkenstocks.

KARYN RUTH WHITE

three hundred? Try out your material on as many sources as you can. If they all laugh, then it's a go; if they don't, then it's back to the drawing board!

Know Your Audience

Another way to minimize the risk of going public with your humor is to know your audience. Obviously, you are not going to have a chance to really know these people, but you can get some pretty good clues about your audience just by asking a few simple questions.

What are the overall demographics of the group? Are they mostly male, mostly female, what is their age range, where do they live? Are they right-wing Republicans or liberal Democrats, or a mix? If you're talking to the Cattleman's Association, that's a different "brand" of humor than the PTA. We've seen speakers and comedians get into trouble with their audiences because they didn't take the time to figure out who they were talking to. One speaker we know got up to speak to a group of dental professionals about cleaning teeth and flossing, but the group he was addressing were all *administrators* for dental practices, not hands-on hygienists. His humor fell flat and he lost the room. KNOW YOUR AUDIENCE! Interview (by phone is fine) at least one member of the group to get some insights that will be invaluable to your choice of humor.

Pre-Schmoozing

If you are a speaker and the group has a social mixer the night before the conference, this is a great place to pick up inside humor to be used in your program the next day. (Always ask the person divulging the humor for their permission to use it.) You can win big points with the

As I've gotten older, my body has changed. Now I have cellulite AND varicose veins! But I don't mind; it gives my thighs that nice quilted look.

COMEDIAN ELAINE BLAINEY

group by doing your homework and personalizing your humor for them. Also, while at the mixer, notice what types of humor the group enjoys. Are they a rowdy group or pretty subdued? Take in as many nonverbal cues as you can to get a feel for the group. This will help you to choose your tone for the next day.

Take it a step further and consider what time you are presenting. If you are up first thing in the morning and they have been partying until late the night before, ease into your humor and perhaps temper your volume. If you are speaking after lunch, they will be more awake and you can afford to be a bit more animated. In fact, this is a great way to get them energized for the afternoon.

Try to get a copy of the meeting agenda beforehand so you know what types of programs are planned. Try to find something humorous about the titles or the content in the agenda. Take note of the sponsors and see if you can weave their names into your stories where appropriate. They LOVE that! (As long as you're not trashing their company.) Also, if at all possible, sit in on the session that comes right before yours so you know what has taken place before you hit the stage. There may be something funny that you can reference, or there may be a topic you want to avoid. You'll also have a feeling for the mood of the room.

Pre-Performance Programming

Thoughts are things. What things do you want floating around in your head before you hit the stage? Zig Ziglar has a great quote about stage fright: "We all get butterflies; the difference is that the pros know how to get them to fly in formation." This is a great quote for putting pre-performance jitters into perspective. You just need to

Friends are God's way of apologizing for our relatives.

UNKNOWN

learn to channel your adrenaline. It's natural, and even healthy, to be a little nervous before you go on. It means you care about what you're doing. If your hands are sweating and your heart's racing, chances are you're doing exactly what you're supposed to be doing.

We all get the pre-show jitters. It's how we handle them that will set us, and our performance, apart. Let your message carry you. Be so passionate and excited about sharing your message with the audience that your excitement overruns any nervousness or doubt.

TRIGGERING PEAK PERFORMANCE

Professional golfers have a routine they use to prepare for each shot. Comedy Improv groups have exercises they do to get their improv minds jump started. Different performers have different techniques for handling pre-stage nerves and getting into a high-performance state. Most successful performers have some sort of ritual they always do before they go on.

In NLP, this is called anchoring; using something you can see, hear, feel, or do to recall a high performance state instantly. Remember your favorite song from your teenage years? The one you always cranked up on the radio? Bringing that song to mind is a form of anchoring. Anchoring is the ability to recall a high voltage state of mind from your past and using it to get your adrenaline going in the moment. Great athletes and performers consistently use these anchors to get themselves "pumped" for their next performance.

As a comedian, one of Karyn Ruth's personal pre-show rituals is to find a way to laugh before she goes on stage. She'll chat and laugh with someone, or she'll think about something funny, or seek out something funny in the

If it weren't for electricity, we'd all be watching television by candlelight.

GEORGE GOBOL

room and laugh. It helps loosen her up and gets her energy centered. She also imagines herself looking down from above as she's getting ready to go on stage. She reminds herself that even though it feels like the biggest thing in the world, she is just one person doing one performance to one group of people. It is not brain surgery. She also reminds herself that she is only the messenger; the message comes through her, not from her. Reminding herself that she's there in the spirit of service helps her to relax, get centered, and tap into the divine power source.

Some performers like to pace before a performance to get their metabolism revved up. Others like to meditate and do deep breathing. Others have affirmations they repeat. When Karyn Ruth is feeling really stressed about a particular performance, one of her affirmations is, "Remember Karyn, this is supposed to be fun. Go have fun up there!"

Take some time before a performance and think about what helps calm your nerves and gets you centered. Remember a time when you were in the perfect state of mind to perform. What did you do to get into that state of mind? What were you thinking, feeling, seeing, hearing, or doing? Find a few key things that you can do minutes before you perform to access your peak performance state, and create a ritual that will anchor you every time.

The statistics on sanity are that one out of every four Americans is suffering from some form of mental illness. Think of your three best friends. If they're okay, then it's you.

RITA MAE BROWN

CHAPTER EIGHT
PERFORMING COMEDY

STAND UP AND DELIVER

Every time Karyn Ruth goes on stage, she thinks of her act as "crafting a comedy quilt." In stand-up comedy, each bit is a series of jokes crafted around a common theme. She sees each bit as a square of the quilt. Over the years she has written a lot of different bits that she can quilt together in various ways. This allows her to create a slightly different performance every night, keeping her material fresh. At the same time, she is willing to step out of the quilt and into the moment if something funny or unexpected happens in the audience. As she's in the moment, she tries to think of a bit she has in her repertoire that she can weave into that particular moment. Each performance, whether it's her stand-up routine or her keynote program, is pieced together out of written and rehearsed material, ad-libs, and in-the-moment improvisation.

PLANNED SPONTANEITY

Unless you're watching *Whose Line Is It Anyway?* or *Hollywood Squares*, most of the comedy you see is written, crafted, and rehearsed, with an occasional bit of improvi-

I don't make jokes. I just watch the government and report the facts.

WILL ROGERS

sation. Even some of the bits used in improvisational comedy are based on a particular formula, giving a basic structure from which to spring ideas.

Some of the great "spontaneous" moments in comedy were planned in advance. Did you know that Paul Lynde wrote all of his material before each taping of *Hollywood Squares*? He was prepared to appear spontaneous. This didn't make his material any less funny; he still wrote it. Didn't it look like he was just thinking up those great lines off the top of his head?

Karyn Ruth calls this "planned spontaneity." This is a wonderful tool to have as a performer. You should always have a cache of funny one-liners or quips that you can use in a variety of situations. That way, even when you're not feeling funny or when you would normally be at a loss for words, you've got a response tucked away in your back pocket that always gets a laugh. Remember Johnny Carson's classic response when a joke would bomb? "Bombo!" Carson became the master of planned spontaneity. He would often tell a joke he knew would bomb because he knew the real laugh was in his response to the bombing.

When something unexpected happens and it gets a big laugh, the comedy mind automatically thinks, "File that away and use that again." This is how comedians (and you) start to build their supply of planned ad-libs. There are very few truly spontaneous ad-libs. Being professional in your performance delivery means being prepared for anything. So as you are preparing your performance, ask yourself, "What would I say if someone spilled a drink? What could I say if someone came in late?" etc. And remember, always allow yourself to be "in the moment" on stage. When you come up with a new line on

My parents visited me in California. While they were there we had an earthquake. I said, "Dad, don't be afraid, its only an earthquake." He said, "Afraid? Hell, I can't wait for the next one. It's the first time your mother's moved in bed in fourteen years.

KARYN RUTH WHITE

stage that gets a big laugh, file that line away and remember it for the next time. That's how you build your comedy quilt.

ATTITUDE

Attitude is your emotional take on a subject, and comedy attitudes run the gamut of emotions from love to hate, ecstacy to fear, insecurity to arrogance. For instance, I *love* chocolate, I *hate* traffic, I *loathe* rude people on cell phones, and I *could care less* about Howard Sterns' next career move, etc.

Presenting your point of view with a specific attitude adds dimension and color to your humor. Think of Rodney Dangerfield, Steven Wright, Woody Allen, or Roseanne. What are their prevailing attitudes? They all deliver their material from one main perspective. Rodney is misunderstood: "I don't get no respect." Roseanne is indignant: "I'm not a housewife, I prefer to think of myself as a domestic goddess." Steven Wright's emotion is no emotion: "What is the speed of dark?" Woody Allen's attitude is neurotic and fearful: "The first time I had sex I was terrified. I was alone."

You don't have to deliver all of your material from just one perspective. Try on a few different attitudes and see which one feels right. Experiment with your delivery by trying your material from a few different angles/attitudes, and see which way sounds funniest.

PROPS

The use of props is a personal decision. In stand-up, "The Prop Comic" was always the guy other comics accused of going for the cheap laugh. You were considered *less than* a real comic if you used visual aids to get a laugh.

All performers get butterflies, but the pros know how to get them to fly in formation.

ZIG ZIGLAR

Karyn Ruth never used props in her stand-up act, but she does use them (sparingly) in her keynote programs. A word of caution when using props: make sure your prop underscores your point and is not merely a distraction or a cheap attempt to be funny. Practice with your props and get comfortable with them before you use them. Don't let the prop become the star of the show; your props should play a supplemental role, not take center stage.

TIMING

Is comic timing something you can learn or is it something you are born with? We believe the answer is Yes and Yes! Like having an ear for music, some people are born with an ear for comic timing; most are not. However, timing, like any skill, is one you can improve through practice.

So how do you learn comic timing? Start by listening intently to the people who do it well.

Exercise:

Tape a stand-up show on The Comedy Channel or one of your favorite comedy shows, or listen to a tape or a CD of one of your favorite comedians, and pick out one routine you like. Play the tape over and over and write the routine word for word in your Seventh Sense Journal. Then memorize it. (Start with a short routine to make this exercise manageable.) Practice imitating the delivery style of the comedian, their pacing and their pronunciation of the words. In essence, become that comedian. Try on the persona of that performer until you can "feel" their timing.

Practice the routine until you have it memorized and you can deliver it like the original. Make notes about what

How many astrologers does it take to screw in a lightbulb? Thirteen. One to screw in the bulb, and twelve to try and figure out which house it's in.

KARYN RUTH WHITE

you liked about the experience and how it felt to try on another comedian's timing.

Note: We are not suggesting that you steal another comedian's material. We *are* suggesting that through this exercise, you will learn how it feels to deliver quality comedy. Then you can extrapolate from what you learned and apply it to your own humor style. All the best performers have "borrowed" tips on style, timing, pacing, gesturing and other performance techniques from others, and then have adapted them to make them their own. So why not learn from the best?

WHAT IF THEY DON'T LAUGH?

Ah, the million dollar question! Have we mentioned that using humor is a risk? Whether you are on stage, at a dinner party or in a staff meeting, using humor is a risk. Our hope is that some of the information and skills you've learned in this book will help to minimize the risk, but there are no guarantees that humor is going to work 100% of the time. That's what makes it hell and that's what makes it fun. So what do you do when they don't laugh?

BOMB'S AWAY

The first time Karyn Ruth went on stage, she totally bombed. "I had no material. I just got up and tried to be funny. My brother and a friend took me out to dinner before my big debut and gave me a rose. They said, 'Karyn, this is your first time on stage and we're so proud of you. You're going to be great.' I wasn't great. In fact, I bombed, big-time. When I sat down, my brother looked at me and said, 'You sucked.' But even after doing it and sucking big-time, I still felt different from the rest of the world. I'd conquered my fear of getting on stage. Now, all

I have had a perfectly wonderful evening, but this wasn't it.

GROUCHO MARX

I had to learn was what to do when I got up there. That took another year of comedy-writing classes and practicing with other budding comics, but I did it.

"After 20 years of writing and performing comedy, I don't have a pat answer on what to do if they don't laugh. I think you have to remember not to take yourself too seriously, and remember that this isn't brain surgery; no one died except you. You know the old saying, 'Never let 'em see you sweat?' I think there is a lot of truth in that. If you tell a joke and it falls flat, move on. Don't dwell on it and DO NOT berate the audience for not getting it. I've heard comedians and speakers say, 'Come on people, that was funny!' This is a surefire way to alienate your audience."

Karyn Ruth compares stand-up to the performance of a concert pianist. Have you ever seen a concert pianist stop in the middle of a performance and say, "Oh, darn, I hit a wrong note; now I'll have to start all over." No, they just keep on playing. So if you hit a wrong note, just keep on playing. If you continue to hit wrong note after wrong note, then you need to go back and learn the music. We've heard many performers blame a bad performance on the audience. If 95% of the time you are a hit and 5% of the time the audience doesn't laugh, then it's the audience. Any ratio higher than that, and it ain't the audience.

HECKLERS

Hecklers are everywhere. They come in all areas of life. Whether you're on stage, working in an office or dealing with customers, hecklers are not far behind. So, what's the best way to handle them?

Karyn Ruth tries to ignore or dismiss them and let that negative energy go right on by. She also tries to have

Some guy hit my
fender the other day,
and I said unto him,
"Be fruitful, and
multiply."
But not in those
words.

WOODY ALLEN

compassion for people because you never know what kind of pain another person is in. However, her compassion only goes so far and then she has to act.

Here's one of her heckler stories (this is the meanest she's ever had to get with a heckler):

"One night in Texas, a very drunk woman was in the front row screaming and shouting while I was on stage. I stopped my show and politely asked her to be quiet. I started up again, and so did she. The second time I asked her to be quiet, I was a bit more firm but still polite. I started again and, you guessed it, so did she. By now the audience was mad and they wanted me to deal with her. I realized at this point that one of us was going down and I decided it was going to be her. So I looked at the audience and said, 'Could you excuse us for just one second?' Then I bent down right in this woman's face and said into the microphone, 'Ma'am, I've asked you twice to be quiet and you've refused. Now I'm not exactly sure what your problem is, but I can guarantee you, it wasn't my house that fell on your sister.' She looked at me like a deer in the headlights and then the audience just lost it, laughing. The bouncer escorted her out, put her in a cab, and the show went on."

As a performer, Karyn Ruth had to take control of the situation, and so do you. When you can, try to handle a heckler with humor and try not to be too terribly mean.

WHAT IF I OFFEND SOMEONE?

Congratulations, welcome to the world of humor. Once again, there are no guarantees as to how people are going to take you. For instance, some women are offended by dumb blonde jokes, while other women think they're hilarious. Using humor is a judgement call. Consider

If you're lookin' to find yourself a good stallion, don't go wastin' your time in the donkey corral.

MAE WEST

your audience before you tell the joke. If you're telling a sexist joke to a woman, chances are good she'll be offended. Remember, when humor comes from a mean-spirited place, it isn't humor, it's ignorance masked as humor.

We believe if your humor comes from a good-hearted place and your desire is to connect with others, not to alienate or belittle them, then your chances of offending someone are less. If you do offend, always apologize immediately and tell that person it was not your intention. Most people understand and are willing to forgive you if your apology is sincere.

We live in a world that is so preoccupied with being politically correct all the time, we're afraid to say anything to each other anymore, let alone attempt humor. We believe that well-intentioned humor is always worth the risk. Life in a humorless world is no kind of life.

KEEPING IT FRESH

Many performers do the same show from one club to the next with very few changes. It is important, whether you are a comedy performer or a speaker who uses humor, to keep your material fresh. The most important thing about keeping your material fresh is that it makes it fun for you. If you're having fun, chances are good that your audience is having fun right along with you.

Mae West was famous for making each performance sound fresh, whether she had done it once or one hundred times. Continue to experiment with your material. Add a new line or a new joke or a new twist to your current material and see what happens. Check in with yourself periodically and ask, "Am I having fun? Am I bored with my material or do I still get excited about presenting it?" Keeping it fresh will keep you energized, and it's so much

If your parents never had children, chances are you won't either.

DICK CAVETT

more enjoyable than "phoning it in." Audiences can sense a presenter who is bored with his own material.

NOTHING BEATS A LIVE AUDIENCE

Okay, you've studied your Humor Heroes, you've written and honed your material, you've done the exercises in your Seventh Sense Journal, you've rehearsed with your humor buddy, and now you're ready to go live. This is the thrilling and terrifying part. We think you have to be a person with a pioneering spirit to have the calling to speak and perform in front of others. We're sure you have to have a masochistic streak to want to perform comedy. Karyn Ruth can say from personal experience that a good night on the comedy stage is a feeling of total exhilaration.

There is a magical dance that happens between a performer and an audience. It's a magic that can't be duplicated anywhere else. It's fleeting, yet unforgettable. When you perform in front of a live audience, try your best to be there. Try not to live in your head the whole time in an attempt to remember your lines. Prepare well and then go have fun. Relax, do your pre-performance ritual to get centered, and then go have a special experience with that audience. This is what makes performing live so special. You have the opportunity to create a wonderful bond with a group of strangers. If you do it right, there won't be a stranger in the room when you're done.

Here's a suggestion: record every performance and then listen to it within 24 hours. This is a wonderful method to use to hear what went right and what still needs work. This is how you become a great performer!

What are the three
most important things
about the afterlife?
Location,
location,
location.

QUOTE ON CHURCH SIGN

CHAPTER NINE
HUMOR FOR SPEAKERS

Using humor as a professional speaker is a different experience with different expectations than using humor as a comedian. Your range of humor subjects is more narrowly defined than a club comic's, and is based on your topic and what is considered appropriate in a business setting. As a comedian who works in the club setting as well as the corporate setting, Karyn Ruth has some insights to share on how to more effectively use humor in your speaking programs.

KNOW YOUR AUDIENCE

As we mentioned in Chapter Seven, *Before You Go Public*, knowing your audience is the first step in knowing what is most likely going to move them to laughter, action and applause. Find answers to as many of the following questions as you can before deciding what type of humor to use:

1. What does your audience already know about your topic?
2. What is your audience's attitude toward your topic?
3. What does your audience do for a living?
4. What is the economic status of your audience?
5. What is the predominant political affiliation?

USA Today has come out with a new survey. Apparently three out of four people make up 75 percent of the population.

DAVID LETTERMAN

6. What is their education level?
7. What cultures are represented in your audience?
8. What is the gender mix of your audience?
9. What is the age range of your audience?
10. How many people will be in your audience?
11. What common bonds unite your audience, e.g., political, professional, family, geographical, societal?
12. What specific stressors has the audience been through that you might be able to address using humor, e.g., a new computer system, merger, overworked, etc.?

PREPARING YOUR PRESENTATION

1. Start early – it gives you more time to enrich your presentation. Take time to reflect on your audience, your message, and yourself. Ask yourself, "What do I want humor to accomplish in this program?"

2. Decide exactly what message you want your audience to receive. Make a list of your key points. If you are a keynote presenter, three key points should be your maximum, and sometimes, if done well, one point is sufficient.

   As speakers and trainers we tend to overload ourselves and our audiences with too much information. We want to "get it all in," and then we rush through our program and the audience suffers. Narrow down your message to three key points and then focus on fleshing out those points with stories, humor, real-life experience, research, etc.

3. For each point, ask yourself, "What's funny about this?" Think of a personal story that could illustrate the point, a joke you think is appropriate, an observation you've made, a third-party story, or a quote. Remember, in order for humor to be an effective tool in

The older I get, the better I was.

UNKNOWN

your program, it must pertain (however loosely) to your point. Bring the audience back to the point once you've used humor. For example: "Isn't this a perfect example of how we ..."

4. Read the local paper of the town you are presenting in (even if it's your hometown) for potential humor. Find out what issues your audience is dealing with, whether it's annoying local road construction or a new Mayor. Here is an example of how Karyn Ruth used this technique in a program:

"I was in Rhode Island and the meeting planner was driving me to the program. We went over a rickety bridge and she told me how the city had built a new bridge but the construction wasn't sound, so they had to go back to using the old, very dangerous bridge until a new one was built. When I got to the event, I opened with the following line: 'I just had a terrifying ride over the XYZ Bridge. It's the only bridge in America where you don't need a token to get across, you need a next of kin.' The audience went wild and I had them for the rest of the program."

People really appreciate it when you take the time to find out what is going on in their lives. It is a wonderful way to warm an audience to you. Once an audience likes you, they are much more receptive to what you have to say. Bob Hope was a master at this technique. He would send scouts to the next city in which he was performing to find out from the locals what was going on. Then he would write comedy based on the information and the crowds loved him. No matter where he went, people felt like he was one of their own. You can create a similar effect.

You grow up the day you have your first real laugh at yourself.

ETHEL BARRYOMRE

MISTAKES SPEAKERS MAKE WHEN USING HUMOR

Here are a few friendly suggestions on what to avoid when using humor as a speaker:

1. The bad segue: The bad segue is any phrase that is an overly obvious transition statement. Avoid using phrases like, "Speaking of ...," "And that brings me to my next point," or "But seriously folks..."

2. Don't attempt to use humor if the company you're speaking to has just been through a bad layoff. If their pain is immediate, they will not be receptive to humor – in fact, they will resent it. Humor is not well accepted right after a tragedy. Think about 9-11. Humor was not appropriate until some time had passed, and then it was accepted only if it was humor against the terrorists.

3. Don't use unrelated humor. Don't start your talk with some unrelated joke just to get them laughing. Start with something that will connect you with the audience, not some formulaic joke that you got off the Internet. It's hack and you don't want to be a hack.

4. Don't step on your laugh. When they laugh, let them laugh. Don't say, "Oh, wait a minute, that's not the funny part." Here's a hint: If they're laughing, that *is* the funny part! This is why it's great to record your programs. You can then go back and reconstruct exactly how you worded and delivered the line that got the unexpected laugh and thereby increase your odds of getting the same reaction the next time. This is how great performers "plan spontaneity."

Life is too short to take seriously.

GEORGE BERNARD SHAW

PUTTING IT ALL TOGETHER

A successful speech has five major components:

1. Introduction: write it for the person introducing you, and write it in a way that guarantees them a laugh!
2. Opening: a short warm-up to connect with your audience.
3. Body: three main points illustrated by stories.
   Point 1 - Humorous Story
   Point 2 - Humorous Story
   Point 3 - Humorous Story
4. Summary
5. Closing

The best formula for connecting with an audience is to be yourself. When using humor, keep it pertinent, keep it real, keep it respectful and keep it clean. Follow this formula and you have a great chance for success.

My father was a
striking man – not
especially handsome,
he just liked to hit
people.

KARYN RUTH WHITE

CHAPTER TEN
CREATIVITY AND HUMOR

When Stanford University authors Michael Ray and Rochelle Myers studied creativity in business, they found five key attributes of the creative leader: intuition, will, joy, strength, and compassion. As Jay studied comedians, he found similar traits. He decided to overlay the findings from The Stanford study as they apply specifically to creating comedy.

INTUITION – THE SIXTH SENSE

As defined by the authors, intuition is "a direct knowing without conscious reasoning." While intuition has been dismissed by some as a viable business tool, the Stanford study found that intuitive leaders outperformed their peers by a factor of two. "The New Jersey Institute of Technology found that eighty percent of those company leaders who had doubled their companies' profits in a five-year period had above-average precognitive powers (intuition)."

For comedians and anyone who uses humor, there also is a direct knowing. It's an intuition about what's funny, without knowing exactly why.

The comedian is the fellow who is wise enough to play the fool.

WILLIAM SHAKESPEARE

WILL

Will is the conscious willingness to take responsibility for one's creativity. Comedians take responsibility for turning everyday experience into creative expression. They have to believe with their intuitive sense that something is funny and follow through with the discipline of crafting humor.

JOY

For all the work and difficulty that creativity entails, it always brings a sense of joy. Being funny is easy, but making a living at it takes hard work. Every comedian will tell you that there is a powerful jolt of joy that comes from crafting a joke that works like magic.

STRENGTH

Everyone needs the strength to break through the wall of fear that might stop them. Where creative business people take appropriate risks, comedians also take appropriate risks, learning to manage their fear of failure and becoming more confident in the strength of their intuitive voice.

COMPASSION

Compassion is a "loving kindness" for yourself and for others. Great comedy belittles no one and elevates everyone.

Studies have shown that there is a direct link between a playful attitude, and productivity and creativity. There is a great deal of stress in life and your ability to laugh and joke will help you relieve that stress, making you more

Chaplin's genius was in comedy. He had no sense of humor.

LITA GREY (Chaplin's Ex-Wife)

productive and less exhausted. You can make life, work, and relationships a terribly serious problem, or you can seek the surprise, delight, and laughter in them.

Why do we get blocked when it comes to creativity? We are probably inhibited by fear, and negative personal judgement and critical chattering in our own minds. To create, as to live, involves risk. Start with compassion for yourself as you begin your creative journey. Start with a belief in your own creative value. Get immersed in the process without overly connecting with the result. Enjoy the act of creating. Start slowly, start small, start safe, but just start!

May you live all the days of your life.

JONATHAN SWIFT

CHAPTER ELEVEN
YOUR COMEDY ACTION PLAN

So at this point you've learned how you can start to increase your comedy awareness. This is the first step in developing a highly-honed Seventh Sense. With practice, the ability to see the funny will become hard-wired into your brain. You'll know it's become hard-wired when something frustrating happens to you and in the midst of your frustration you stop and ask yourself, "What's funny about this?"

You've learned exercises to help you jump-start your creativity, including how to use associations to create new connections, and how to plug into a standard formula (e.g., The Top Ten List) to create humor quickly. You've learned how to use attitudes and different points of view to bring dimension and color to your humor delivery.

So ... what are you going to do with all of these new insights and this newfound knowledge? In this chapter we want to recap the key points of the book and help you create a Comedy Action Plan to get you started on your way to developing a highly-honed Seventh Sense.

JUMP-START YOUR SEVENTH SENSE

If we had to distill the process into three steps, they would be the following: Hilarity Begins at Home, Get it Down, and Get a Second Opinion.

It's never too late to have a happy childhood.

ANONYMOUS

HILARITY BEGINS AT HOME

Make a commitment to turn on your comedy radar and start asking yourself, "What do I think is funny?" You have to think something is funny before you can show other people the humor. Who or what in your life do you find hysterical? What about yourself do you think is funny? What observations about life in general tickle you? Keep these questions in mind as you go through your daily activities.

Watch people. Hang out in an airport or a mall. People are hilarious. Just sit in the park and watch kids play. You don't have to watch kids very long before you're cracking up.

With enough practice, you will get to the point where you're not even conscious that you're looking for the humor in daily life. That's because you've plugged in your scanning software. You'll listen to conversations differently, you'll perk up when you hear something funny, or you'll see a person in the grocery store as a funny character instead of a weirdo. You'll learn to push your own humor buttons and feel that flood of endorphins. You could become a humor addict.

Learn from the comedians you like and avoid the ones you don't. Go to your favorites often and drink from the humor well, because life can drain your well very quickly. Call upon those friends who make you laugh until you cry, and if you don't have any, get some. Part of honing your Seventh Sense is making it a priority in your own life to say, "I need a humor refueling!"

GET IT DOWN

Have a process in place for recording your funny observations and ideas. These are fodder for future funny stories. Whether you carry a small notebook with you at

I'm not afraid of death.
I just don't want to be there when it happens.

WOODY ALLEN

all times or use a micro-recorder, get it down! Write key words that will trigger your memory, and don't edit, just record. This will help you when it comes time to sit down and write comedy. Rather than staring at a blank page, you will have this jumping off point.

If you find something in the paper or on the Internet that you think is extremely funny, save it and share that with your circle of friends. Catch the comedy in life. Stop and say, "That was funny." Write it down. Remember it. Repeat it.

Listen to the words people say and ask yourself, "Is there another way to take what they just said? Is there a double-meaning that I can explore to get a laugh?"

Relax, be yourself, be playful. Start with an attitude of, *I'm going to relax. I'm going to be in the moment. I have a couple of stories that I think are funny and I'm going to unleash them on the world and let whatever happens, happen. I'm not going to force it, I'm going to naturally make myself open to a really playful, fun attitude.* A funny thing happens when you live with this attitude. People begin to sense your sense of play and they'll come to you with their funny stories because they know you're open to humor.

GET A SECOND OPINION

Find a Humor Buddy. Team up with someone you trust and practice writing and delivering material together. The more people you can "trial run" your humor with, the better you'll know how it's likely to be received by an audience. If people tell you that they don't think it's funny, LISTEN! It's better to bomb in front of one person than three hundred. Hey, no one ever said that being funny was going to be easy!

You can trudge through life, or you can laugh and sing and dance! The days go by just the same.

UNKNOWN

IT'S UP TO YOU

Misery is not our natural state, but some of us are brought up to think it is. Whether you trace it back to your religious upbringing or your parents' beliefs about life, the message we often get is that there is nobility in being miserable. We grow into adults who believe that if we aren't miserable, then we're not busy enough.

Think about it, have you ever walked down the halls of your office and said, "I'm totally caught up." No! You wouldn't even dare to say that. Because immediately your boss would say, "Well, obviously, you don't have enough work to do." We wear overtime and overwork as a badge of honor in this society. This is the type of thinking that pharmaceutical companies love! What wacky thinking!

Step back for a minute and think about the statistics on stress-related illness in this society. It is out of control and it's time for a new attitude.

Remember, children laugh over four hundred times a day, while adults laugh a mere fifteen times. Give yourself permission to learn from children and make it your mission to reclaim some of your lost laughs. You can trudge through life or you can laugh and dance and sing ... the days go by just the same. Have a happy life!

When my mother was in a bad mood, she'd bake.

She used to let us lick the beaters ... sometimes, she'd even turn 'em off first.

KARYN RUTH WHITE

CHAPTER TWELVE
COMEDY BOOT CAMP

OPEN-MIC NIGHT

Almost every city in America has a comedy club or bar that offers an open-mic night for fledgling comedians. They are usually held on a Monday or a Tuesday night long after most people have gone to bed. Though not easy to do, these are excellent opportunities to test your material (and courage) on stage.

In the words of Frank Sinatra, "If you can make it here, you can make it anywhere." The goal as a club performer is to get your humor out of your head, off the written page and out of your mouth in front of total strangers. Gauge their reaction, rework your material, and then go do it again.

LIZARD SKIN

What's the goal? You'll need to develop skin as tough and impenetrable as a lizard's, because you've only got two minutes to make people laugh. And you're going to bomb sometime. It might as well be early in your career.

And don't think you can just walk in and walk on. There's a waiting list. The Comedy Works in Denver gets requests from 80 people a week for 10 to 15 slots, so it may

The higher the hair, the closer to God.

TEXAS WISDOM

take several weeks to get on. And you may get bumped if a well-known comedian wants to try out new material.

Comedy Darwinism

Survival of the fittest. Open-mic night separates the stand-ups from everybody else. It's not for everyone, but if you're thinking about a career in comedy, it's a great training ground. And if you're love of comedy outweighs your fear of failure, you'll develop the lizard skin and comedy persona that's right for you.

Get out there! Make us laugh! The world needs you!

KARYN RUTH WHITE

Karyn Ruth White's calling is to help people live with more laughter. As an active member of the National Speakers Association, she is a professional speaker and comedian with a positive message and a hilarious style. Karyn Ruth started her comedy career performing stand-up across the country for 12 years, and she's been presenting stand-up and humorous keynote programs for over 20 years. She delivers her presentations with a positive punch and she is positively hilarious.

Karyn Ruth's gift is the ability to connect with people on both a humor and a heart level. She takes information that will help people live better quality lives and she wraps it in humor. People connect because they're laughing, they're having a good time, and all the while, the information is getting in. That's how Karyn Ruth uses the gift of humor.

Karyn Ruth is the owner of Laugh and Learn Productions. She travels around the world teaching people how to use humor for stress management and to better cope with life. A lot of people come up to her and ask, "How can I bring more humor into my life? How can I put more humor into my presentations?" So she and Jay brainstormed on how to combine their talents to teach anyone how to use their Seventh Sense and this book was born.

"Comedy is my life's calling. I love the sound of laughter, my own and yours. I love to see people shed their worries of the day and just laugh with abandon. I love the sound of the little sighs people make after they've had a good laugh. I love watching them wipe tears of laughter from their eyes. I love performing. I love laughing with the audience. I love cracking myself up. I love it all. This book is my way of sharing my love for comedy, humor, laughter and joy of spirit. This book is a gift of love from me, my co-author, and the comedy muse."

For Keynote Programs:
Contact Karyn Ruth White at 1-877-KRWHITE or visit www.karynruthwhite.com

JAY ARTHUR,
the KnowWare® Man

Jay Arthur is a speaker, trainer and consultant. He works with companies that want to plug the leaks in their cash flow and people who want to master the mysteries of the mind. He is a long-standing member of the National Speakers Association. Jay spent 21 years with the phone company working with hardware and software, slowly going nowhere. Then he began to study how we run our "big brains" using what he calls KnowWare® – software for your mind: studying pictures, sounds, things that we say to ourselves and our feelings.

Jay became interested in Neuro Linguistic Programming (NLP) and, as a master practitioner, he's learned to reverse-engineer the software of the mind. By studying people as they talk about how they do something effortlessly, he can determine how people (like Karyn Ruth) run their brains to produce outstanding results in the world. About five years ago, Jay took one of Karyn Ruth's comedy classes; he wanted to learn how comedians think.

Jay studied Karyn Ruth and how she thinks about creating humor. What are her filters? What does she believe? How does she take a simple, normal activity and make it funny? How does she take the dark underbelly of everyday life and make it funny? Jay also studied other humorists and comedians from the National Speakers Association. Virtually any time he saw somebody talking about comedy, he watched and listened. He began to grab onto what they were saying and figured out that all comedians do pretty much the same thing. They all run their minds in basically the same way. His research and expertise will help you understand how to get the same kinds of results that comedians do.

Also by Jay Arthur:
> *How to Motivate Everyone,* LifeStar, 2003
> *The Motivation Profile*, Lifestar, 2004.

For Consulting or Training Programs:
Contact Jay Arthur at 1-888-468-1537 or 303-756-9144
knowwareman@mindspring.com
www.motivateeveryone.com
www.qimacros.com

Imagination is more important than knowledge.

ALBERT EINSTEIN

Resources

COMEDY BOOKS

Carter, Judy, *Stand-Up Comedy*, Dell, 1989.
Carter, Judy, *Comedy Bible*, Fireside, 2001.
Fletcher, Leon, *How to Speak Like a Pro*, Random House, 1996.
Goldberg, Natalie, *Writing Down The Bones,* Shambhala, 1986.
Perret, Gene, *Business Humor*, Sterling, 1998.
Perret, Gene, *Comedy Writing Step by Step,* Samuel French, 1982.
Theibert, Philip, *How to Give a Damn Good Speech*, Career Press, 1997.

NLP BOOKS

Arthur, Jay, *Motivate Everyone*, LifeStar, 2002.
Arthur, Jay, *The Motivation Profile*, LifeStar, 2003.
Connor, Joseph, *Introducing NLP*, 1990.
Dilts, Robert, *Modeling*, NLPU, 1998.

The purpose of our life is happiness.

DALAI LAMA

Want a positively hilarious program for your next meeting?

Visit national speaker and comedian
Karyn Ruth White online at:
www.karynruthwhite.com

Want to learn how to think like a comedian?

Consider hiring Jay and Karyn Ruth to train
your team or association members.

Visit online at:
www.yourseventhsense.com

For more products from Karyn Ruth or Jay, visit www.yourseventhsense.com

NOTES

NOTES

NOTES